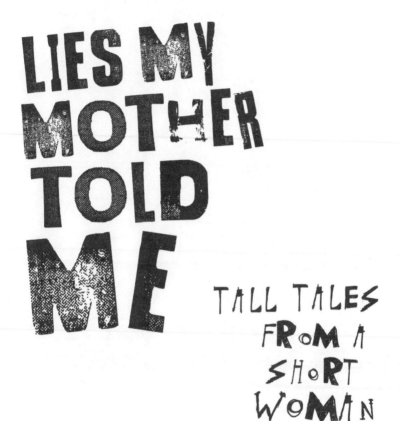

LIES MY MOTHER TOLD ME

TALL TALES FROM A SHORT WOMAN

MELISSA RIVERS

Post Hill
PRESS

A POST HILL PRESS BOOK

Lies My Mother Told Me:
Tall Tales from a Short Woman
© 2022 by Melissa Rivers
All Rights Reserved

ISBN: 978-1-64293-740-4
ISBN (eBook): 978-1-64293-741-1

Cover design by Cody Corcoran
Interior design and composition by Greg Johnson, Textbook Perfect

Post Hill Press
New York • Nashville
posthillpress.com

Published in the United States of America
1 2 3 4 5 6 7 8 9 10

To Cooper...
Sorry about this.

Mark Twain once said,

*"If you always tell the truth,
you don't have to remember anything."*

Where is Mark Twain today? Dead.

Perhaps honesty isn't the best policy.

Disclaimer

Satire is a genre of the visual, literary, and performing arts, usually in the form of fiction and less frequently non-fiction, in which vices, follies, abuses, and shortcomings are held up to ridicule, with the intent of shaming individuals, corporations, government, or society itself into improvement.

In 2020, right before the COVID pandemic began, I was having lunch with my friend Sandy, a book editor, at a quaint beachfront restaurant in Santa Monica. We were chatting about this and that, when somehow the subject of lying came up. (Maybe because C-SPAN's live coverage of Lindsey Graham speaking was on the TV behind the bar?) Have I mentioned that my mother and Lindsey had a few things in common? The only ones I'm legally allowed to mention are lying and an expansive shoe closet. I began regaling Sandy with some of the gazillion lies my mom told me through the years.

All of a sudden, in the middle of a story, Sandy put her hand up and yelled, "Stop!"

I said, "What? Did I cross some #metoo line I wasn't aware of? Do I have spinach in my teeth? Am I bleeding from the ears because I'm having a brain hemorrhage?"

"No, no, no," said Sandy. "This is more than lunchtime talk; this is a book!"

I said, "Oh, thank God; I'd hate to have spinach in my teeth. You really think this is a book?"

She said, "Absolutely!"

I said, "Would you edit it?"

She said, "Absolutely not! You know I'm fearful of the legal system, that's why I only edit true crime books; most of the people are dead or in jail. Both of which make it difficult for them to be litigious. But I'll send you the number of the perfect, possibly drug-addled editor. Be aware, she responds best to texts."

She did. And so the writing began.

Not only was writing this book lots of fun, but it was also surprisingly easy. "How's that, Melissa?" you ask. "Is it because you have a photographic memory like Harry Lorayne, the world's foremost memory expert?"* Thank you for asking, and no, I do not have a photographic memory, but I do have a good memory. I also have my mother's journals, letters, and the hate mail she never sent. Due to the quarantine, stay-at-home order (which, quite frankly, had nothing to do with the quarantine—idle hands are the devil's workshop), and lack of anywhere to go, I had the luxury of sitting in my home office (aka my bed), day drinking and writing this tome. So, every story, tale, lie, and conversation in this book is exactly how I remember it.

---

* Harry Lorayne is an author, magician, and memory expert. He's written lots and lots of books on memory and memory training. I say "lots and lots" because I don't remember exactly how many books he's written.

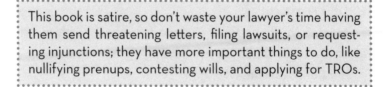

This book is satire, so don't waste your lawyer's time having them send threatening letters, filing lawsuits, or requesting injunctions; they have more important things to do, like nullifying prenups, contesting wills, and applying for TROs.

Contents

Introduction

In today's world of fake news, alternative facts, truthiness, and "truth-adjacent," lying is all the rage. It's the twerking of 2021. We all know that politicians, publicists, criminals, and children lie. A lot. But no one, no one lies with the passion, creativity, and chutzpah of mothers. I should know—I'm a mother. And I had a mother, Joan Rivers, who was almost as good at lying as she was at comedy. She turned lying into an art form; she was the Picasso of prevarication.

> *Joan:* "Melissa, you'll be fine during natural childbirth. You don't need drugs. It will be the most wonderful moment of your life. I should know; I had natural childbirth with you."

> *Truth:* She took forty Valium, sixty Seconal, had a morphine drip, and downed a fifth of vodka in the car on her way to the hospital. She didn't wake up until I was seven.

That lie she told me changed my life forever. I had natural childbirth. My son is twenty-one now, and I still resent him for putting me through that pain. A couple of milligrams of Xanax when he was crowning, and we would have a much better relationship today. Just sayin'.

The little house where I grew up, in a tiny village called Bel Air—or, as I like to think of it, the scene of the crime. Four beds, four baths, and twenty-six panic rooms.

Careless Whispers

"Melissa, I was thinking about our conversation the other night, you know, the one about you breaking up with your boyfriend because of sexual dysfunction. Anyway, Margie thinks that..."

"What do you mean 'Margie thinks'? You weren't supposed to tell anyone!"

"I didn't."

"You told Margie!"

"Of course, I told Margie. She's my best friend."

"Mom, I asked you not to tell anyone!"

"I didn't."

"Then how does Margie know?"

"No clue."

"Did it come up in conversation?"

"Maybe."

"Did you say anything?"

"Not a word."

"So, let me get this straight; Margie, out of left field, apropos of nothing, casually said, 'So, Joan, do we know of anyone who dumped her boyfriend because he couldn't get it up?'"

"Yes. But I didn't tell her."

"Mom, I specifically told you not to tell anyone."

"I didn't."

"You told Margie!"

"Well, of course I told Margie. She's my best friend. She would have found out anyway."

"How? How would she have figured it out anyway?"

"Because of you. You know you can't keep a secret, Melissa. You unfortunately have one of those faces that tells the truth."

"*I* can't keep a secret? Why in God's name did you think it was okay to tell Margie?"

"Oh, I see, we're back to Margie."

"Yes, we're back to Margie. Because I told you something personal and told you not to tell *anyone*, and you told Margie."

"Melissa, stop carrying on. You knew I would tell Margie. I ONLY DID IT FOR YOU. *You* told me because you knew I would tell her and you wanted her to know."

"Why would I want Margie to know about my boyfriend's sexual dysfunction?"

"How would I know? I'm not a shrink."

"Did Margie tell anyone?!"

"Melissa! Of course not! Margie knows how to keep a secret."

"Good, then next time I have to secretly confide something very personal and very important to me, I'll go to Margie."

"Fine. Be that way."

"I will!"

"Go right ahead. Talk to Margie. She'll tell me anyway."

Uncle Robert

I come from a large Jewish family—or should I say, I was "born into" a large Jewish family. There's a big difference. Let me explain. "Coming from" a large Jewish family means many children and I would have lots of siblings. I'm an only child. Therefore, I was "born into" a large Jewish family. That means lots of aunts, uncles, cousins, and in-laws (some of whom we like and some of whom are "Can you believe she married that idiot? For what, he doesn't even have money?").

Most modern Jewish families[1] have two children. TWO. Not three, not four, TWO. If you see a Jewish woman with

---

[1] When I say "modern Jewish families," I am excluding the Chassidic Jews because modernity is not their thing. My mother never understood *how* the Chassids had so many children. "Melissa, no disrespect, but they're not a sexy bunch. The women wear dowdy clothes, chunky heels, and cheap wigs."

"Why do they wear the wigs?"

"Because their husbands think if other men see their wives' real hair, they won't be able to keep their hands off of them...I know, I know, it's crazy. I've always wanted to say to them, 'Excuse me, fellas, I've seen your wives without their wigs; I can assure you, no one's going to get all handsy with them.' Also, Melissa, the men are more than a little on the repulsive side. They wear black in the summer, heavy coats in August, crumbs in their beards, ecch."

"Mom, that's a really broad generalization."

"Really, Melissa? You want to hook up with Zev Feinberg, the four-hundred-pound Chassidic man known as 'The Zipper King of Flushing'?"

"Eeww, no."

"I rest my case."

more than two children, you can bet that at least one of the extra children comes from a first marriage.

It wasn't always like this. A hundred years ago, Jews, like everyone else, had lots of children. In middle school, we learned about the great migration of the Irish and the Jews, who came to this country at the turn of the twentieth century in search of better lives. This should not be confused with the great Asian migration of the 1970s, when the Japanese and Chinese came to this country in search of colleges with good math departments. (Education is the key to success, my friends, so no need to wonder why China is now leading the world in everything...they value education! Their kids are in school studying and learning while we have Goober in a truck, huntin' and drinkin'.)

One fact that stayed with me after I graduated eighth grade was that all of those turn-of-the-century immigrants had lots and lots of children. It was not uncommon for a woman to have ten or eleven children. In those days, if a woman only had six or seven children, neighbors would titter behind her back that she was "prudish" or "barren." It was also not uncommon for a woman to rent out her uterus as a storage space for seasonal furniture.

My great-great-aunt Gertie, who was born in Romania in 1889 and came to America when she was five, had ten children, three miscarriages, and an abortion. My grandmother would always ask, "Gertie, you were pregnant for twenty years; didn't you and Uncle Max ever go to a movie?"

At one point, I asked my mother why women had so many children in those days.

She said, "Fluoride, Melissa, fluoride."

"Fluoride? Mom, what the fuck are you talking about?"

"In 1900, the drinking water didn't have fluoride, so many of the women had rotten teeth, all cracked and chipped and broken. Which meant they couldn't give blow jobs, which meant they had to *shtup* a lot. And *shtupping* leads to babies. And having babies depletes a woman's calcium supply, which makes teeth even worse, which then leads to more *shtupping*. The worse the woman's teeth, the more children she had."

"Are you out of your..."

Interrupting, as usual, she continued, "...Missy, remember the Old Woman Who Lived in the Shoe?"

"Yeah...?"

"If her teeth had been any worse, she would have had to move into a thigh-high boot with all of those whiny little brats. Mona Lisa? Remember her? Why do you think she wasn't smiling? 'Cause she was grumpy? 'Cause she was a sourpuss? No! It was because she *couldn't* smile. You see, Mona only had two molars, a jagged incisor and a rogue wisdom tooth. Looked like a Halloween jack-o-lantern. That's why Mona Lisa didn't have any children. If her teeth were better, she would've had a gaggle of kids. Right? Wrong. Because Mona also had periodontal problems which gave her such bad breath that no man could get within fifteen feet of her. Leo DaVinci was way, way across the room when he painted her. In fact, he had to have his assistant, Jerry, take a couple of Polaroids of Mona and tape it to his easel so he could do the fine detail work without getting into sniffing distance of her. "

"Really? Is that true?"

"Melissa, would I lie to you?"

"Yes."

"Another reason women had so many children in those days was that the children had to work to help support the family, but due to disease and famine a lot of children died, so the parents had to have understudies to step in and pick up the slack."

"Understudies? Like in *All About Eve*? You're equating dead children to a Bette Davis movie?"

"Oh, don't be ridiculous, Melissa! It's more like *Pride of the Yankees*, the movie about Lou Gehrig, starring Gary Cooper. I'll tell you the story."

"Mom, I'm a sports fan. I know the Lou Gehrig story."

"Yes, but you don't know the real story. Besides, I tell it better."

Knowing I was in for the long haul, I lay down on the couch and covered my head with a pillow, hoping it would just pass.

"In the early 1920s, the New York Yankees had a first baseman named Wally Pipp. Wally was good, not great, but fine. Like an opening act in Vegas, he did the job. He was the Freddie Roman of baseball. One afternoon, Wally wasn't feeling so well, so he goes to the manager and tells him he can't play because he has a headache. So the manager puts in his understudy, Lou Gehrig. And you know what?"

Like an idiot, I asked, "What?"

"Wally Pipp never played again. Starting that day, Lou Gehrig played 2,130 straight games. Fourteen years the man didn't take a day off! Amazing; I thought Betty Buckley was a workhorse, putting on that heavy *Cats* costume and singing and meowing on Broadway eight shows a week, but that Lou was something else. At first, I figured it was because of his Teutonic bloodlines, but then he got sick and died at thirty-nine, so there. Did you know that Lou Gehrig was anti-Semitic? That's why he hated Babe Ruth."

From under my pillow, I yelled, "Mom! There is no evidence anywhere of Lou Gehrig being anti-Semitic! And what in God's name would that have to do with him hating Babe Ruth? FYI, Babe Ruth wasn't Jewish."

"I know that Melissa, but Lou didn't; he was dumb as a bag of hammers. He thought Babe Ruth was named after Ruth, from the Bible. Ruth was a *shiksa* but married an Israelite, which makes her Jewish-by-injection. Hence, the alleged anti-Semitism.

"You know, the best thing about Lou Gehrig was that he died of his *own* disease. How fabulous is that? Lou Gehrig died of Lou Gehrig's disease! Do you think they'll ever name an illness after me?"

"They already have, Mom: Crohn's Disease."

"Uh! That is so hurtful, Melissa. And to think, I breast-fed you."

"No, you didn't."

"Well, I thought about doing it once when the nanny was giving you formula, but I was wearing a new Chanel blouse.

Anyway, just like a cheap massage parlor, the Lou Gehrig story has a happy ending."

"How?"

"Well, it wasn't happy for Lou, but it was happy for Wally Pipp. After losing his first base job to Gehrig, Wally quit baseball altogether and reinvented himself. He became one of Gladys Knight's backup singers, even though he was white."

"Mother, that is not true."

"It most certainly is, Melissa. Wally was a Pip. If you don't believe me, ask Gary Cooper."

"You knew Gary Cooper?"

"We had an affair. We were lovers. Go ask him."

"I can't; he's dead."

"Then ask Gladys Knight. She's not; she'll tell you. Go ask her."

With that, my mother walked out of the room. I remained. Which somehow leads me to Uncle Robert.

I don't know exactly how I'm related to Uncle Robert; I just know he's somebody's son or somebody's brother on somebody's side of the family. I also have no idea where he is these days, but I'll get to that in a minute. In my family (as is the case in many families, I suppose) there were a lot of "aunts and uncles" who weren't really aunts and uncles, but just close friends or business associates of my parents. I had lots of aunts and uncles I was in no way related to. There were Aunt Eleanor and Uncle Murray, Aunt Elsie and Uncle Bill, Aunt Jean and Uncle Al. These were my parents' "card friends," people they played cards with at the country club on Wednesdays and Sundays, but who I called Aunt and Uncle for as long as I can remember. When I was in high school, I finally came to the realization that these people—all of whom I loved—were not actually my blood relatives. We were studying genetics in my biology class when I realized that there was no way my Aunt Jean was a blood relative of mine. For starters, she was Jamaican and could play a mean steel drum. I was doing a homework assignment on recessive genes when the light bulb went off. I stormed into my parents' bedroom and said, "So...Aunt Jean. Not really my aunt, is she?"

My mother looked up from the Lillian Vernon catalogue she was reading and said "Well, of course not, Melissa. What are you, stupid?

"Of course, she's not a blood relative. And neither are Al or Eleanor or Murray or Elsie or Bill. When you were born, they all loved you so much, we considered them to be your extended family and knew that, God forbid anything ever happened to us, they would all take care of you."

"Mom, wow. I'm shocked; that is so sweet. I love them too. They truly are part of our real family."

"Oh please, Melissa; if they were real family, they'd be in the will...and they're not. I love them, they mean the world to me and your father; but they're not getting a fucking dime when I go toes up."

So, back to Uncle Robert. Robert was one of my favorite uncles, and not just because he actually *was* an uncle, but because he was the "cool uncle." He was the uncle who got you high, told dirty jokes, and taught you how to flush your drugs without clogging the toilet. He was my gay uncle. Except nobody would acknowledge it. No one ever said the word, "gay," which was so weird, especially given that 83 percent of my mother's audiences, acquaintances, and friends were gay.

I figured out Uncle Robert was gay when I was seven or eight. He was babysitting one night, and I decided I wanted to play with my Barbie doll. So I went into my room, put her hair in a chignon, and dressed her in a beautiful, gold evening gown. I ran back into the living room to show Uncle Robert. I said, "Uncle Robert, look; look how I dressed Barbie!"

I was expecting him to say something like, "That's beautiful, Melissa," or, "Love her hair, sheer perfection!" What I got instead was a long pause, a slight *tsk, tsk,* and, "Flats?"

I was so upset I began to cry. Uncle Robert put his arm around me and said, "Let's turn that frown upside down" (which I'd heard my mother's plastic surgeon say to her three months earlier).

Uncle Robert continued, "Flats are for informal, casual occasions. They go well with sundresses, culottes, or Capri pants, à la Mary Tyler Moore on *The Dick Van Dyke Show.* Evening gowns require something a little more formal, maybe a sling back or a stiletto, provided it doesn't cross the line between striking and slutty."

"Did I ruin Barbie's outfit completely?"

"Don't be silly; of course not. It could have been worse; you could have put her in a corrective shoe. C'mon, you silly goose, take a deep breath and dry your tears. I'm not going to tell your mother. Let's go to the kitchen and have ourselves a nightcap. I forget, do you prefer an olive or an onion in your martini?"

In those few minutes, I realized that Uncle Robert was different, but in a great way. The next morning, I spoke to my mother as she made breakfast (and by that, I mean she hovered over our longtime housekeeper, Betty, while *she* made breakfast).

"Uncle Robert is so great," I said. "How come he's not married?"

"Because he's musical," my mother said.

"Musical?"

"Yes, musical."

I knew she was lying. And she knew that I knew she was lying. (Even at that young age, I'd heard euphemisms for the word "gay," like "flamboyant," "light in the loafers," or "that old queen can really suck a mean dick," but, strangely, never "musical.") So, I thought I'd catch her in the lie.

"So...I guess that means Boy George is 'musical,' huh?"

"Of course not. Have you ever heard him sing?"

I last heard from Uncle Robert about six months ago. I got a postcard from him from Sweden. It read, "M, Been an eventful year. Lots of changes. Meeting Caitlyn in Mykonos for a vacay. Talk soon. Muah! —R"

Only the Lonely

When I was growing up and found out that I wasn't adopted, I was crushed. My heart broke knowing that I was the product of those two bickering things in the kitchen. What was even more distressing was that I was an only child; I had no brothers, no sisters, not even a conjoined twin, who might hamper my mobility but would at least give me someone to talk to.

I can't tell you how many times I asked my mother why I was an only child. In the beginning, she gave me a variety of answers, all steeped in love and insincerity:

1. "We wanted to give ALL of our love to you."
2. "You were perfect, and we knew we couldn't do any better."
3. "I didn't want to share you with anybody."

When those answers no longer worked, she became more "honest" in explaining why I didn't have any siblings:

1. "Your father doesn't touch me anymore."
2. "Too expensive; your upbringing is bleeding us dry."
3. "It's hard to pass off two sets of stretch marks as a belt."

My mother and I just got back from shopping. ☺ *My father just got the bill.* ☹

On my thirteenth birthday, I found a letter from my mother on my pillow. I guess she decided I was mature enough to hear the real story as to why I was an only child. She told me the story of Adam and Eve—actually, it was one of multiple stories she told me about the World's First Couple (see page 88, "The Garden of Eden").

Dear Melissa,

Okay, the truth—why you're an only child. This is going to take a minute, so pull up a chair and pour another glass of white wine, and I'm going to tell you the story of Adam, Eve, and Eve's cunty sister, Debbie.

I always found the story of Adam and Eve in the Garden of Eden puzzling. For starters I could never figure out why, when they had the entire planet to themselves, did they choose to live in a stifling hot, barren desert with no air conditioning. Why not a lovely beach town or a shady, pine forest? First rule of real estate: location, location, location!

Second, the notion that Eve was created from Adam's rib is ridiculous. Admittedly, most men want to put a bone inside a woman's body but this is not what they're actually talking about.

Adam and Eve had two sons, Cain and Abel. Cain was a farmer and Abel was a shepherd. I know, I know—what kind of jobs are those for Jewish boys? When's the last time you heard anyone at Temple Beth Am say, "Oy, my son, the shepherd; I'm so proud"? Couldn't have been a dentist like his cousin, Elliott? Anyway, the boys got into a fight and Cain killed Abel. Took him out to a field and left him there. It's like an episode of Dateline except without the guy with the deep voice.

So, after that bit of sibling ugliness, Adam and Eve were down to one son, and not even their favorite. This made them sad and lonely. After months of sitting in bed, eating Fritos and staring at cave-drawings, Eve decided to have another son as a replacement for Abel; his name was Seth. (Ironically, years later Seth found himself in a similar position as a "replacement player," when he became a stand-in for the second Darrin on Bewitched.)

Anyway, after the annoying fratricide incident and the arrival of Seth, the First Couple decided that they should expand their family more and had many other sons and daughters, including an orange one named, Donald.

Things were going fine in the Garden of Eden and every-one was happy until one afternoon—a Tuesday, I think—Eve, began inexplicably day drinking as well as becoming high-strung and unpredictable. Perimenopause, perhaps? Shortly thereafter she took the advice of a snake and ate an apple, "the forbidden fruit," and the rest is history. (FYI, contrary to what many biblical scholars believe, the fruit was not forbidden by God, but by Dr. Alan Fleckman, Eve's gastro-enterologist, who had her on a gluten-free, low-fructose diet, in an effort to ease the effects of a duodenal ulcer.)

If you're wondering, "What kind of an idiot listens to a snake?" Remember: I work in show business. What most people don't know is that "snake" is the Aramaic word for "agent." Anyway, Eve wasn't just listening to some garden variety garden snake. Oh no, the snake she took advice from was not just some slithering a-ped waiting to be turned into a handbag, but a professional snake who used to run the television department at WME. The snake was trained by Eve's covetous sister, Debbie. That's right, Missy, Eve had a sister people rarely talked about, in much the same way the Jackson family rarely talks about Rebbie.

A little backstory: Debbie was known in the family as "the smart one," which was a nice way of saying she had a mustache and a hump. Debbie was jealous of Eve and that Eve had such a handsome baby-daddy, while she, the "smart one," was left to build bookcases, work on her golf swing, and was relegated to being the "fun aunt" at holiday gatherings. So Debbie devised a plan to get Eve out of Eden. Turns out

Debbie was an avid reader and one night, while perusing a copy of Snake Fancy magazine, the light bulb went on. Debbie went out and found a local rattlesnake and taught him to speak. And quicker than you can say, "Try an apple; what could go wrong?" the snake had Eve chomping away on a nice, ripe McIntosh. (Actually, it wasn't quick; due to his forked tongue and severe underbite the snake spoke with a pronounced lisp and it took forever to get, "H-h-he-e-l-l-o thexy; howya' doin' hot thtuff? Intretheed in a delithoius thnack?" out of his venomous mouth.)

(According to the snake's mother, "If he'd have just worn the goddamned retainer his teeth wouldn't have shifted back and we wouldn't have pissed away all that money on braces.")

Within five minutes of eating the apple, God, using a loophole in the lease, evicted Adam and Eve and their litter of young'uns from the Garden of Eden and sent them all to live elsewhere. Some went east, to the Land of Nod, while others went west, to Boca Raton, where Dr. Fleckman had a satellite office. Conniving Debbie, who must have had some dirt on God, stayed in Eden and took over Adam & Eve's condo, which she, and her "gal pal," Pat, renovated in Dutch farmhouse style.

Long story short: If Adam and Eve had just had the one son, and made Cain an only child, NONE of the other crap would have happened; Adam and Eve would've have stayed in Eden, Cain wouldn't have killed anyone, and Debbie would still be nothing but a husky PE teacher living outside of Madison, Wisconsin.

THIS, my darling daughter, is why you're an only child. My child. Who I love more than anyone. Ever.

Xoxo
Mommy

PS—Truth be told, you were supposed to be a twin, but you ate your sister in utero. Why do you think I'm always bugging you about your weight?

Working the Strip

Years ago, my mother and I were in the back of a limo, driving down the strip in Las Vegas. At some point, she turned to me and said, "Melissa, there are only two types of women who work the Las Vegas Strip: hookers and me."

"What's the difference?"

My mother paused, trying to figure out if I was simply naïve or if I was being snarky beyond my years. She decided it was the latter and replied, "The difference, sweetheart, is hookers won't leave you alone and penniless in the back parking lot of Caesars Palace. I will."

This conversation took place when I was in sixth grade and my mother was performing in Vegas. Why she thought I'd understand what hookers were at that age might be baffling to you, but not to me. You see, when my mom was on stage at Caesars, I was usually in the bar bending an elbow with Bambi, Muffin, and Bubbles, *n'est pas*? I learned *a lot* from those gals. For example, if a man seems to have a speech impediment, it's probably because he's hiding a wedding band under his tongue. Or if a man says he wants to go "around the world," it actually has nothing to do with travel. And the most important thing? Never carry cash! Why? 'Cause if you don't carry cash, you can't make change!

Las Vegas is one of the most interesting, exciting, and preposterous cities ever built, whether seen through the eyes of a child, an adult, or a performer. There is no place quite like it, although my mother swore that she knew of a co-ed prison that had many of the same features. How she knew this, I do not know; there are some questions even I wouldn't ask.

Las Vegas is not really a "kid-friendly city," even though it went through a "Disney phase" in the early 2000s, when they (city officials, civic leaders, CEOs, and a coupla leftover mobsters) were trying to turn it into a family town. They built water parks and candy stores and theme parks with rides and ponies. But it didn't work because, in Vegas, the only ponies people cared about were the ones they were betting on, and the only rides they got were on Bambi, Muffin, and Bubbles.

But I was a kid who spent a lot of time in Las Vegas and I really liked it. Of course, I didn't do most of the adult things: gambling, drinking, vomiting in the lobby, trying to figure out how you wound up naked in the coffee shop at the Sahara... you know, that kind of stuff. I did normal kid things like organizing meet-and-greets, hawking tickets on the strip, fending off subpoenas, and hanging out with bikers at tattoo parlors.

The main reason I loved Las Vegas was all of the cool people I got to meet. My mom and dad's list of show biz friends was pretty vast, ranging from the sublime to the fabulously ridiculous.

Take magicians for example, both sublime and ridiculous! Vegas was chock full o' magicians. There was Lance Burton, his ex-girlfriend Melinda, "The First Lady of Magic," David Copperfield, and of course, Penn & Teller, who remain my friends to this day.

I remember the night I met Melinda, The First Lady of Magic. After her show, which was great, I asked my mom, "Is Melinda really the First lady of Magic?"

"No, of course not, Missy. Eleanor Roosevelt was the First Lady of Magic; she fooled Franklin into thinking she wasn't a dog. Sleight of hand? Try sleight of face."

"Then why do they call Melinda the First Lady of Magic?"

"If they called her 'The Thirty-Seventh Lady of Magic,' would you buy a ticket? Of course not. Besides which, she *is* a fabulous magician; she made Lance Burton disappear. One day, Lance is her hot, magician boyfriend on the cover of magazines; the next day, he's a pair of threes at a one-dollar table in Binion's Casino."

"Wow! Is that true?"

"Did you like the story?"

"Yes."

"Then what difference does it make?"

I was—and still am—a huge David Copperfield fan. His tricks are amazing. When I was going to meet him, my mother reminded me not to call him a magician.

"Why not?"

"For the same reason you don't call a proctologist a doody-handler. He finds it demeaning. He prefers 'illusionist.'"

"What's the difference?"

"How the fuck should I know? I'm a party clown; I put on a fancy dress and make strangers laugh. I think illusion is just magic on a much grander scale. Bigger tricks, bigger paychecks! David's worth four *billion* dollars. You don't make that kind of money pulling handkerchiefs out of your sleeves."

"Was Grandma a magician? She always had handkerchiefs sticking out of her sleeves."

"No, she was in a touring company of Mummenschanz. Don't ask, you're not going to get the joke. That's a reference only three people on the Upper West Side of Manhattan, all gay men named Jonathan, will get, so don't waste your time."

Anyway, as our limo pulled into the parking lot of a nice restaurant where my mother could eat for free, she gave me a big hug and said, "Melissa, I have a surprise for you; today we're having lunch with my friends, Siegfried and Roy."

"Really, Mom? Wow! That is so cool! I love them, even though I can't tell them apart."

"Siegfried's the tall blonde, Roy's the little one with the whip. They're lovely...really sweet, funny guys; you'll like them."

"Are they a couple?"

"Yes...in the same way that Uncle Robert is musical. But to the public, no. They live together, they work together, they travel together, and they bathe together, but to the public, they're just a pair of straight, wacky, German friends putting on a show."

"Mom, I'm only eleven and I don't believe that for one second; no way the public doesn't think they're a gay couple."

"I agree, Missy, but *they* think that no one knows and that's all that really matters. In much the same way that Mama Cass of the Mamas and the Papas didn't think she was fat. She believed she was as hot as Michelle Phillips and equally as fuckable, which was, of course, not true. But because Cass believed she was hot, it made her a better performer and gave her an air of sensuality that appeals to men far beyond traveling salesmen who buy fetish magazines. Add that sensuality to her fantastic singing voice, and you can see why she was a big star. And I mean big. Truth be told, without Cass Elliott, the Mamas and the Papas would've just been three musicians on food stamps, smoking weed in a filling station bathroom."

As we got out of the limo, my mother grabbed my arm and said, "A couple of quick things, Missy. Number one, do not comment on how tan they are; they spend every waking moment lying in the sun. Siegfried is three weeks away from looking like a handbag."

"Why do they do that?"

"They think having a tan makes them look thinner. Roy once told me that he thinks melanoma is a small price to pay to look nice."

"If they want to look thinner, why don't they just purge, like everyone else in show business?"

After a scolding pause, my mother said, "Everyone?"

"Oh, I'm sorry; I mean everyone in show business *except* Mama Cass."

"That's my girl! You are so present! I'd give you a kiss, but I don't want to ruin my lipstick; just imagine I'm being affectionate. Number two, they're German. Try not to mention Hitler, Goering, Nuremberg, or *Kristallnacht*; it makes them twitchy. And number three, whatever you do, don't order meat! Even though they work with lions and tigers, they love *all* animals, including cows. The sight of a burger or a steak makes them weep."

Siegfried and Roy were already there when we arrived, and my mom was right—they were nice and sweet and very funny...for a few minutes...until I accidentally ruined the meal. The server came over to take our orders; the boys had green salads and my mother ordered Altoids and soup. Then came my turn. I wanted to sound cool, like I belonged at the table with all of the grown-ups, so I said, "Could the chef throw a piece of salmon in the oven?"

Silence. DEAFENING SILENCE. Then, as one, Siegfried and Roy let out a couple of high-pitched shrieks and began sobbing. They jumped up, grabbed their man-purses, and ran out of the restaurant faster than Jesse Owens at the Berlin Olympics.

I was shocked. "Mom! I am so sorry! I wasn't thinking. I shouldn't have mentioned ovens."

Our server jumped in to calm me down. "It's not the ovens, young lady; the crematoriums don't bother them in the least. It was the salmon that set them off."

"The salmon?"

My mother got that "oh my God" look on her face and said, "I forgot. Melissa, this isn't your fault; I should have told you not to order fish either. Siegfried and Roy used to work with a giant porpoise named Carol. Roy and Carol were very close. Until one fateful day, when Carol died in a freak accident. An empty bottle of Man Tan got caught in her blowhole and she choked to death. The boys have never gotten over it, especially Roy. To this day, when a Bumble Bee tuna ad comes on the TV, he has to take two Valium and go lie down for a couple of hours."

Lest you think I destroyed not only a meal but also a friendship, think again. My mom was right—Siegfried and Roy were sweet and kind. Later that night, they sent a gift bag to our hotel room, filled with snacks and candies and bottles of wine, along with a note that said, "Dear Melissa, so sorry we behaved in such a silly manner. Hopefully you can forgive us. You're such a beautiful girl; if you were twenty years older one of us would surely want to go out with you."

The snacks and candies were delicious, the wine (according to my mother) was superb, and the note was...well, delusional. But, if *they* believed it...

Melvin

As birth records show, I am an only child. I've often said that even though I was an only child, I wasn't my mother's favorite—her career was her favorite child. But something I've neglected to mention is that for years, and I mean *years*, I believed I had a brother.

Because my mother *told* me I did.

I was somewhere around the age of nine. I was relatively bright, but not yet the sophisticated arbiter of taste I am now. I understood basic kid things, like "do your homework," "eat your vegetables," and "brush your teeth." But I was nowhere near understanding "residuals," "back-end points," or, "There is no way I'm paying that sonuvabitch a commission; he didn't do anything." (That came when I was twelve.) And I certainly didn't know anything about biology, genealogy, or the state adoption laws in New York and California.

I had taken an interest in art and drawing, and I was in our hotel suite with my pens and pencils, doodling in one of the Wonder Woman sketch books my father had bought for me, over my mother's objections. "Edgar, Wonder Woman?

For Melissa? Are you crazy? Wonder Woman's way too butch. I don't mind the bulk jewelry and primary colors, but the man-hands and what appears to be a codpiece in her shorts? No."

It was an early summer day in Las Vegas, and we had just come in from the pool, where my father was working a tan and my mother was making disparaging comments about the woman sitting a few feet away from us. "Melissa, look at that lady in the orange bikini. But only for a second—I don't want to traumatize you. It's like an eclipse; you never look straight into it because you'll get glaucoma or retinitis pigmentosa."

"What's retinitis pigmentosa?"

"Don't know, don't care. I imagine it has something to do with the eyes and vision. Tony Randall is their spokesman and Tony told me they're paying him a small fortune to represent them. I should do something like that, you know, become a celebrity spokesman for a disease or a rash. Imagine me as The Face of Colitis! Ka-ching!

"Anyway, don't ever become that woman sitting over there on the lounge chair."

"Why? She seems nice. She's not bothering anybody."

"Nice? Not bothering anybody? She's bothering everybody who doesn't have retinitis pigmentosa. For starters, she's way too old to be wearing a bikini. Bikinis are for young women, like we see in those tampon commercials on TV. They're young and gorgeous and running on the beach and swimming and diving and boating."

"That sounds like fun; can I get some tampons?"

"Can you? You'd better; Daddy bought stock in Kotex. Anyway, that woman is at least fifty, way too old to be flashing her *pupick*. Even worse, she has stretch marks, which means she's either had children, or she's an ex-Olympic weightlifter. But look at those arms; she puts the f in flabby. The only thing she's snatched and curled is a Big Mac. And don't ask me what a snatch and curl is until you're at least thirteen.

"This woman's also got *a lot* of stretch marks, so either she's had a couple of babies—or one huge baby that came out of her like a giant turd the day after a Passover Seder.

"Melissa, if I teach you but one thing in this lifetime, let it be that if you have even one tiny, visible stretch mark, it's time for a one-piece, a sarong, some body makeup...or time to stay the fuck indoors."

"I don't understand. Why is covering up stretch marks so important?"

Shocked by my question, my mother lost her balance and stumbled backwards, only preventing a fall by grabbing on to the wheelchair of a man next to her, who was either sleeping, comatose, or dead. (Have I mentioned that my mother always liked to position herself near the handicapped when in public places? Why, you might ask? Because, "You always get better service when you sit near the infirmed. Waiters come over every five minutes to check on them, to make sure they're doing okay, either out of a healthy-person's guilt or fear of discrimination lawsuits." I can't tell you how many times a maître d' has said, "Would you like a table near a window, Miss Rivers?" and my mother replied, "No, I prefer a table near someone blind, withered, or being spoon-fed by a caregiver."

Anyway, back to the woman at the pool. "Melissa, men don't want women with stretch marks, especially when there are plenty of women without them. To a man, dating a woman with stretch marks is like buying a car...a used car. It still runs, and it still looks good, but there are a couple of dents here and there, and you know something weird has gone on under the hood."

"What about the Osmonds? Mrs. Osmond has lots of children and the husband is still with her. She must have a lot of stretch marks."

"A lot of stretch marks? Her stomach looks like an accordion. But it turns out Mr. Osmond loves it. When he goes down on her, he can play 'Lady of Spain' with his tongue. I'm sure after the first coupla kids he had a case of buyer's remorse, but by that point it was too late for a trade-in; she had depreciated too much to have any market value. So, they made the kids go out on stage and perform like circus animals.

"You know, Missy, I've always wondered how Mrs. Osmond manages to walk down the street and not just leak all over the place. I mean after all those kids, she must have some pretty loose lips. Forget leaking, I'm surprised she hasn't accidentally passed a kidney or a lung."

"You've *always* wondered this? This is what's on your mind?"

"Okay, not always. Sometimes I wonder about how conjoined twins go scarf shopping. Anyway, one more thing about the woman in the bikini, before I forget. When she stands up, her pooch hits the floor. Everything drops when you get older, Melissa. When the woman gets up from her lounge chair, and you hear 'kerplunk,' that's her vag hitting the pavement."

I have digressed way too much here; sorry. So, up in our hotel suite, I'm working on my Wonder Woman book when my mother says, "Aren't you a little old to be drawing? Shouldn't you be in college or something?"

I said, "Mom, I'm nine."

She said, "Oh, I'm sorry, I forgot. It's just that I got spoiled by your brother, Melvin."

And then she turned and walked out and headed into the bedroom for her daily, post-complaining nap, leaving me sitting there, dumbfounded.

"MOM! What brother? Who is Melvin?"

I ran into the bedroom in a panic. By the time I got there, she had already "forgotten" the bombshell she'd just dropped on me.

"Hi, honey. What's on your mind? Wanna watch TV?"

"Who is Melvin?"

She motioned for me to come sit on the bed near her (not next to her, near her. I guess she didn't want to feel compelled to hug me if I broke down). "Sweetheart, I never told you because I didn't want to hurt your feelings. You have an older brother named Melvin whom you've never met because he was so smart, I had to put him in a special school for extremely gifted children. He's still there, and he's doing great, straight As, reading two grades ahead. Thank you for asking."

I was stunned. "Mom, are you telling the truth? Is this real? How did I not know this?"

"You know who would've known this? Melvin. Because he's not only smart, he's intuitive."

"Why didn't you tell me?"

"What, and make you feel like an idiot? I didn't even tell your father."

"Daddy doesn't know he has a son named Melvin?"

"He's not Daddy's son, Melissa. I had him before I met your father. I mean, Daddy's smart, but not Melvin smart. And before you ask, no, he's not my first husband's son either."

"Then whose son is he? Mom, you have to tell me."

Long pause. Then, "$E=mc^2$."

"What?"

"$E=mc^2$. If you were reading instead of drawing, you'd know. It's the theory of relativity by Albert Einstein. Do you know who Albert Einstein is?"

"The genius, right?"

"Yes, the genius; good girl."

"Albert Einstein is Melvin's father? You dated Albert Einstein?"

"Not dated, more like friends with benefits. I remember the way his eyebrows tickled my thighs..."

"MOM!"

"Ah, the memories. Anyway, my beautiful, wonderful, B-plus student daughter, Melvin is still away at the School for Geniuses. Maybe someday, when you're old enough to handle the disappointment of having recessive genes and knowing he'll always be the smart one, you'll meet him.

"But until then, you be you. You're beautiful, you're nice, you have a great personality. Besides which, men don't like really smart women."

"Einstein liked you."

"As a friend."

"I don't know what to make of all this."

"You know who would know?"

"Melvin?"

"Melvin. Now, can you call down to the front desk and see if my bikini is back from the dry cleaners?"

Every now and then, after my mother and I had one of our discussions about her penchant for lying (usually on Sundays, which she believed to be a day of reflection—as long as it reflected well on her), she would write me a note and leave it on my pillow to read before I went to sleep. Which does, to some extent, explain the insomnia I've suffered since 1970.

The notes were never about her lying; they were about other people's lying. Sometimes the notes were critiques, sometimes homages, but they were always written without any foundation or logic.

LIAR

WALT DISNEY

Dear Melissa,

You know how Disneyland is called "The Happiest Place on Earth." BIG FUCKING LIE! My gay hairdresser, Jason, says it's the sauna in the Yankees' locker room.

Disneyland is not even close to being the happiest place on earth. I can think of a lot of places that are happier. For example, Tiffany's on its annual 50 percent off sale day, or the gynecologist's office when the doctor says, "No worries, you're just late," or when the probate attorney says, "He left everything to you." Disneyland is an amusement park filled with hundreds of rides, thousands of screaming (mostly unattractive) children, dozens of annoying vendors, huge mice (Mickey and Minnie), and needy actors wearing enormous fur heads playing Snow White and the Seven Dwarfs. (Can you see *that* resume? "I have range—I played both Doc and Dopey...") All day long, these highly trained thespians wander around Disneyland, going from ride to ride taking pictures with antsy, sugar-loaded children.

Sometimes they get the opportunity to participate in "character brunches." Do you know what character brunch is? Of course you don't. Your father never took you to Disneyland. Because we love you. A character brunch is an overpriced buffet where Disney "stars" like Goofy and Dumbo plop their fat asses down into your already overcrowded booth, make stupid faces at the toddlers, mooch French toast off your plate, and make you feel ashamed for drinking mimosas out of your hip flask, in order to not become a Dateline special, "Mothers Who Kill."

Let's talk Mickey Mouse for a second, shall we, Missy? For starters, he only has three fingers on each hand. (No, I'm not mocking the disabled. You know full-well that for seven years I lived with a man who had one leg. Seriously. The sex was great—the parking was even better.) Admittedly, Mickey's three fingers are gigantic and could be quite useful in the proper romantic setting, but do you really want a hulking, deformed rodent sitting at a breakfast booth with Cooper? I'm guessing not.

My big concern is the dwarfs—are we still even allowed to call them "dwarfs;" isn't "little people" more PC? I'm not joking, Melissa, I'm asking an honest question; "dwarfism" is a condition, a genetic mutation that cruelly leads to health issues and life challenges. Disneyland Dwarfs are played by adults, so they're all tall. And "tall dwarf" is an oxymoron, like military intelligence, or "real housewife", or talented Kardashian. Then there are the dwarfs' names: Grumpy, Doc, Sneezy, Sleepy, Dopey, Happy, and Bashful; instead of having normal names like Seth and Jeff and Alan, the dwarfs are named for their various personality traits. How is this okay? In real life, are we allowed to do this? Am I allowed to call my neighbors in apartment 5F, Dave and Arlene, Full-of-Shit and Old Whore? And how do we know that Happy really is happy? Maybe Doc just prescribed an anti-depressant for him and he is only whistling while he works because he's hooked on Adderall? And why are there no dwarfs of color or LGBTQ+ dwarfs? How cool would it be to replace Sneezy and Bashful with Shaquille and Lady G?

Speaking of white...what about Snow White? Walt Disney wants us to think she's a beautiful, virginal princess, but that's not what I see. I see a sexually frustrated woman who, after surviving the New York dating scene, opted for a polyamorous lifestyle in the suburbs, embracing her suppressed lust for little people. ("When I said I wanted seven inches, I didn't mean one at a time.")

Shifting gears...and what about the rides, Melissa? Most of the rides at Disneyland go up and down or upside down, or they spin, turn, and revolve at Mach 11 speeds, which means the children are not only screaming, they're vomiting. Everywhere. All over the rides, the grounds, their friends, and most importantly, you. Disneyland is the place where simple Chanel ballet flats go to die. I've spent enough time in the company of bulimic supermodels that I've been doused with more than my fair share of vomit.

Obviously, the children aren't vomiting solely because of the rides. Once you enter the gates of The Magic Kingdom, every fifteen feet or so, you'll find a restaurant, cart, truck, kiosk, or vendor selling some sort of food product that is a) fattening, b) unhealthy, and c) within ten minutes will cause immediate vomiting and explosive diarrhea. You will spend at least part of your day entering the gates of the Magic Toilet.

Then there are the LINES. There are more lines at Disneyland than on a coffee table in a crack house in the Valley. They're longer than R. Kelly's rap sheet. The only lines I want to see are lines of people buying tickets to my show.

If Walt Disney really liked children, would it be like that? Would it?! No! It wouldn't. Why am I the only person who sees the hypocrisy?

If Walt really liked children, the "Happiest Place on Earth" would have sleep stations on every waiting line, free coloring books, tablets, and toys, diaper and pull-up stands, Ritalin-laced ice cream cones, and most importantly, for the parents—open bars and "put your child up for adoption" lawyers, on site.

You know, Melissa, I think all this craziness was because Walt Disney had some serious Mommy issues. Think about it. Name one Disney movie where the mother didn't die, the stepmother wasn't evil, and the handsome prince didn't look like he spent more time in the closet than the castle.

Happiest Place on Earth? My ass.

Tomorrow we're going to Tiffany's, they're having a sale.

XOXO
Mommy

White Lies Matter

According to Wikipedia, a white lie is a "harmless or trivial lie, especially one told in order to be polite or to avoid hurting someone's feelings or stopping them from being upset by the truth. A white lie also is considered a lie to be used for greater good (pro-social behavior). It sometimes is used to shield someone from a hurtful or emotionally damaging truth, especially when not knowing the truth is deemed by the liar as completely harmless."

A common example of a white lie being used to shield someone from a hurtful situation? Telling a death row prisoner that he's been pardoned and then killing him in his sleep. A win-win. The state is happy, the guy had no idea that his last meal was his last meal. (Unless, of course, all he was offered was a three-minute egg, in which case he might've sensed something was amiss.)

Here's a white lie everyone reading this understands: When a woman asks the question, "Does this dress make me look fat?" the answer is always, "No." If she's morbidly obese and the dress is so tight, it's more of a casing than a dress, the answer is still, "No." (Please note: I am not fat-shaming anyone here; I'm simply justifying little white lies.) Most women aren't asking the question because they want an honest answer; they're asking because they want a jolt of confidence and reassurance that they look good when they go out. Trust me on this. I'm a woman. If a woman wants an *honest* opinion on how she looks, and if "the dress makes me look fat," she'll ask her gay stylist or her best gay friend. Because a gay man will tell a woman the truth...and almost always in a catty-yet-fun, borderline mean way. For example:

Me: *"Does this dress make me look fat?"*

Cary: *"Not if you stand next to the Hindenburg."*

Catty, funny, a little mean...and thank you.

Conversely, there are white lies that women are obligated to tell men. Most of them, of course, are about sex.

"Melissa, always tell a man he's good in bed. *Always.* I don't care if his performance was worse than Colin Farrell's in *Alexander*; I tell him he was great. Not so much to protect his feelings—he doesn't know you're never going to fuck him again—but as I've told you, your generosity of spirit is the door to his generosity with jewelry."

"But what if I AM going to marry him or live with him? We're definitely going to have sex again; why tell him he's good? He'll only want more."

"Au contraire, Melissa, au contraire. Tell him he's so good, so overpowering, so much man, that you're exhausted, and need to rest. Tell him you can't wait 'til next month when you're fully recuperated and rarin' to go again! His ego will be so stroked, he won't care that his penis isn't.

"And speaking of penises, Melissa...always let men think that they're more well-endowed than the Rockefeller Foundation, even if they're not. Which they're usually not."

"Mom, a man knows how he's hung. They're not all idiots. A guy knows if he's got the dick of death or a teeny weeny."

"Not necessarily. Men are delusional when it comes to their bodies. Think back, Melissa—we've taken family vacations to Europe. We've seen all of those fat, bald, repulsive men in tight Speedos, strutting their stuff on the beach like they're Michelangelo's David. The truth is, they're not even as hot as Larry David. But they *think* they are. So even if an ugly guy has a baby gherkin, let him think he's got a giant kosher dill."

"Seriously, Mom? If I go to bed with a man, and instead of having a decent package it's like, 'here comes Thumbkin,' what am I supposed to say?"

"You say nothing, but if you have to say something, go with something like, 'Take it slow, Myron, I'm not used to a man like you.' He'll think you're complimenting him. And it's not really lying, because unless you've slept with a child or a little person, you probably haven't been with anyone like him before."

"Really. And you know this, how?"

"When I was younger, before you were born, I spent quite a bit of time with circus folk. Turns out, little people find me hot. And so did one bearded lady, but we can talk about that another time."

My mother believed that little white lies were "one of God's gifts, like a small nose, a big bank account, and a healthy disdain for chipper news anchors." ("Melissa, no one wants a cheery voice reporting the burning down of an orphanage or the discovery of a puppy-kicking competition. Except maybe for Katie Couric, but she has issues.")

One of my favorite little white lies is, "Thanks so much for the dinner invite, but we have family plans this weekend." It's a lie that's specific enough to be true, and not interesting enough to render it disprovable. FYI, I learned this not from my mother, but from watching every episode of *Law & Order* at least five times. (To this day, I pride myself on knowing every cast and character change, in chronological order, that took place during the series' entire twenty-year run.) On *L&O*, defense lawyers and prosecutors are always advising witnesses to say as little as possible on the stand (especially during cross!) lest they perjure themselves or say something incriminating that could get them in trouble. Stick to the facts and give short, concise answers. For example:

D. A. Jack McCoy: "Did you see the defendant shoot the woman in front of the bodega?"

Witness (good answer): "No."

Witness (bad answer): "No, because I was on my knees giving the defendant a blow job at the time. My back was to the store and I couldn't see his hands because his balls were in my eyes."

One of the most important and *necessary* white lies we all tell is when we encounter friends or acquaintances with a new baby...specifically, an ugly new baby. No decent human being is going to say, "Good God, Lois! What'd you do, fuck a monkey?" Because a) it would be rude, and b) what can Lois say? "Why, yes, Melissa, I did. I got really shit-faced one night and woke up in the zoo..."?

My mother taught me that even legally blind parents who have birthed ugly babies surely are aware of the fact that the product of their loins is anything but a beauty.

According to my mother, "The considerate ones will take the pressure off of you by acknowledging their baby's unfortunate looks before you have to say anything. They'll say things like, 'We know; we're hoping she'll grow out of it,' or, 'Yes, that's a tail, but we think it will eventually dry up and fall off,' or, 'We know, we know; please God, let her be smart, or at least handy.'"

In 2001, two of my most attractive friends gave birth to what I can truly say was the ugliest baby in the history of the world. If you don't believe me, call Ripley's and ask them; they'll tell you. To this day, he's the standard bearer for what-the-fuck-happened. It's been twenty years and, like Joe DiMaggio's fifty-six game hitting streak, it's a record that may never be broken.

He was a happy, healthy, homely baby and, I'm glad to report that, today, he's a happy, healthy, homely adult...and he's also rich! He's made a fortune as the "before" photo in plastic surgeons' offices all across this great land.

Speaking of plastic surgery—a topic you may have heard my mother was familiar with—there are a whole host of white lies we tell people who've had a little nip 'n' tuck...or in the case of Caitlyn Jenner, shock 'n' awe.

Not unlike grief, there are stages of plastic surgery recovery. If Elisabeth Kubler-Ross applied this to herself, she'd have had a much better sex life and been invited to way more Hollywood parties and swanky literary salons. The lies we tell change as the recovery process goes on.

Stage one of Plastic Surgery Recovery, or PSR (I think I've coined an acronym! Yay!), is: Terror. The first time the bandages come off and the doctor hands you a mirror is nearly as scary as finding yourself naked in a sweat lodge with Kevin James. I remember my mother telling me, "Melissa, the first time I saw my new nose, I was shocked. I thought, my God, I look positively Christian! My new nose was so tiny I couldn't figure out how a) I'd ever be allowed into Temple Beth-Shalom again, or b) how I'd ever again be able to snort cocaine off of a toilet seat in a public men's room." (Luckily, she was able to do both.)

I also remember the first time I was old enough to visit my mother in the hospital after one of her plastic surgeries. I think I was eleven or twelve. Or maybe thirty-seven. I mean, honestly, they all kind of blend together. I walked into my mother's room and there was this thing, lying in the bed, gauze wrapped under her chin and around her head. I thought, "This is either Gloria Swanson or Gunga Din." (I was a very advanced twelve-year-old.) All I could see, sticking out from the bandages, was this tiny, little nose. It didn't look human; it looked like a mildly deformed, uncircumcised penis. I said, "Mom, is that you? How are you feeling?"

From under the gauze, my mother mumbled something that sounded like either, "I'll be fine, sweetheart," or, "I paid for a private nurse, where the fuck is she?"

The doctor came in a few minutes later and began unwrapping all of the bandages. Like an artist unveiling a painting, he pulled off the last piece of gauze with a flourish to reveal his masterpiece—a battered, bruised, and swollen Joan Rivers, smiling through the abrasions. If I didn't know this was my mother, I'd have bet the house it was some homeless person who blew an orderly to get a bed.

At that moment, the lying skills I'd learned from *mi madre* came in handy.

"Melissa, tell me the truth. It's awful, right?"

"No, not at all. You don't look that bad. In fact, considering you just had the surgery a few days ago, I'd say you look pretty damned good!"

"Seriously? Good enough to go out on a date?"

What I wanted to say was, "Only if the date has 20/4,000 vision," but what came out of my mouth was, "Maybe tomorrow or over the weekend; you'll probably have trouble chewing for a few days, and you don't want to dribble down your dress."

"I love you so much, Melissa. Thank you for being so honest. Come, give me a kiss."

"Not on your life, Lumpy. If you're lucky, maybe I'll hug you when the scabs fall off."

The second stage of PSR is: Healing. You've been home about a week and the swelling is going down, the bruising is dissipating, and your face is finally beginning to take on proportions that won't frighten small children or Holocaust survivors. You've stopped eating through a straw, your mouth and jaws are working again, and you can blink with only mild discomfort. The problem is that the psychological healing is lagging behind the physical healing and you've developed the face version of body dysmorphia, also known as "facial fuckedupia." (Okay, I don't know if that's really true, but a) it works for me, and b) this *is* a book about lying, so what's the problem?) Facial fuckedupia is when you think you look better than you do. When my mother got to this stage of recovery, I'd find myself saying things like, "Getting close," or, "Wow, almost there," or, "A few more days!" My favorite? "Melissa, can you see the bruising through the makeup?"

"Not really, Mom, although I think a little more concealer might help...a little more...a little more...no, a little more... gooood."

Of course, what I'm really thinking and really want to say is, "Fuck yes, you can! Hey, I've got an idea! Why don't you get on the phone and call the Benjamin Moore people, and I'll run outside and get the garden hose and spray nozzle..."

The third and final stage of PSR is: I-Think-I'm-Ready-to-Be-Seen! This stage usually occurs about ten days or so before it should. Most people who have work done can't wait for the recovery period to be over so they can get out of the house and go out in public once again. These same "most people" usually go out about a week before they should, when they're almost completely healed but not quite. There are still telltale signs that "something looks different," like a droopy eye, a lazy lip, a wayward nostril that sneezes to the left, or the patches of raw skin from the laser resurfacing. It's also during this stage that the person who had the plastic surgery does the lying. My mother's philosophy on this was brilliant: if anyone asks if you've had work done, "Deny, deny, deny, and blame your appearance on some illness, accident, or disaster." For example:

> *Neighbor:* "Joan, you look different; have you had work done?"
>
> *Joan:* "Oh, no, no, no. You haven't heard? I was in a terrible house fire. Ran back in and managed to save three children, the invalid grandmother, and the injured dog (long pause, wipe fake tear from eye). My only regret is that I couldn't save Blinky."
>
> *Neighbor:* "Oh my God, Joan! I never would have known. What a story. You look amazing! Fantastic! So sorry about Blinky."
>
> *Joan:* "Thank you so much. Please don't tell anyone; I'd hate for people to think I'm a hero."

My mother never had the heart to mention that Blinky was an old, broken-down, flat-screen TV that kept flickering on and off.

This *isn't* to say that little white lies don't sometimes have negative consequences. For example:

I have a friend in New York City named Eve. She's a great jazz singer and we met years ago when she was singing backup for a musical star who was a guest on my mother's daytime TV talk show. (I can't remember exactly who it was, but I think it was either Eartha Kitt, Kenny Rogers, or Bananarama; they're all so alike, they blend together.)

Anyway, Eve and I hit it off in the green room and became friendly. Whenever I was in New York, we'd get together and hang out. At least we did for a couple of years. But we started drifting apart because Eve was constantly late for *everything*: work, play, dinner, theater, sports events...it made no difference, she was never on time. And after a while, it started getting annoying. I missed the first five minutes of at least six Broadway shows and the first two innings of nine major league baseball games.

And Eve's excuse was always the same: "The subway was running late." I'm sure that some of the time that was true, but most of the time she was lying...the subway wasn't running late; she just didn't budget her time properly. Maybe she got tied up on a phone call, or she couldn't decide on what outfit to wear, or she mistimed her ex-lax and just couldn't get out of the bathroom. Whatever, it really doesn't matter.

After a couple of years of the constant lateness and constant lying, I'd had enough. And since, like everyone's favorite euthanizer, aka Dr. Jack Kevorkian, I'm solution-oriented. I knew I had to do something. First, I made my meeting times with Eve earlier than necessary to accommodate her lateness, but that didn't work; we still missed the opening of movies and shows. Then I arranged that I'd wait for ten minutes and, if she was late, I was leaving and going about the evening without her. My mother thought that my waiting around for Eve was a terrible idea: "Melissa, if a woman is standing alone on a street corner for more than five minutes, people think she's either homeless or a hooker." Turns out

Mom was right...I got three propositions, twenty-six dollars, and a couple of sandwiches.

Be that as it may, I finally decided I just couldn't make plans with her anymore and stopped seeing her.

Long story short, when I was visiting New York last winter, I ran into Eve on the street:

Eve: "OMG, Melissa, you look great! It's been forever. How long have you been in town?"

ME: "Five days."

Eve: "How come you didn't call?"

Me: "The subway was running late."

Mic drop. End scene.

The "subway was late" lie is the New York version of LA's "I was stuck in traffic" lie, which is one of the most dependable white lies you can tell in California...mostly because it's true. Anyone who's ever been to Los Angeles has experienced the traffic firsthand and won't question the veracity of your excuse for being late.

The city of LA is basically a huge, sprawling suburb—it's about 477 square miles (not including smaller cities that are actually in the middle of LA proper, like Burbank, West Hollywood, and the Scientology Center) and runs from the ocean to the mountains to the valleys to the desert. Laid out end to end, it's longer than a cash register receipt from CVS. It used to be (in the olden days) that to go anywhere in LA took twenty minutes, door to door. Whether you were driving crosstown on the freeway or to the 7-Eleven around the corner, it was always twenty minutes. Now, with soooooo many more cars, but the same number of roads, it takes an hour to go anywhere. At least. Which is really terrible if you've only got fifty-nine minutes to live. (Seriously, do you really want to die sitting in traffic, stuck behind a tricked-out Range Rover with a bumper sticker that reads, "I Brake for Publicists"? I think not.)

Anyway, I'd like to continue writing this chapter, but I can't—I have plans with my family.

The Birds and the Bees

When I was about eleven years old, the most important thing my friends and I learned at school wasn't math or science or history, but sex: baby-making, to be precise. Or at least we thought we were learning...what we were really doing was giggling, starting rumors, and exchanging false information amongst ourselves, not unlike the Trump White House. By that age, I realized that there was no actual stork involved in the baby-making process, but I was waaaay short on the actual details of what really took place. So, one day, after an incredibly imaginative gossip session on the playground with my best GFs, I ran home, burst into the house, and yelled out at the top of my lungs, "Mom, I want to know the facts of life!"

My mother was shocked—believe it or not, explaining sex to me was more difficult for her than buying retail—as was our neighbor, the Widow Feinberg (whose husband had died unexpectedly the day before in a freak bass fishing accident[2]), who was trying to get through her grief by crying

---

[2] Yes, Jews fish.

on my mother's shoulder. (Obviously, my mother was not wearing Armani that day; no one ever cried on Armani.) Mrs. Feinberg began sobbing uncontrollably, got up, air-hugged my mother, and left. I started crying too because I thought my question had upset her, but my mother calmed me down immediately by saying, "It's not you, Melissa; it's her. Mrs. Feinberg's always been a whiner."

Feeling better, I got right back on course. I plunked myself down on the couch in the den (the living room was only for company...*good* company, not whiners like Mrs. Feinberg) and again said, "Ma, tell me about the facts of life!"

"Okay Melissa, here we go. Tootie was the gossipy girl who was wise beyond her years. Natalie was the stocky, Jewish one with the great personality and thick legs. Blair was the pretty WASP who, deep down, probably hated Tootie and Natalie, because...well, you know. And Jo was the 'troubled' one who seemed way too mannish to be on network television. And Charlotte Rae played Mrs. Garrett, a role I should have had, but the network wanted to go with a dumpy redhead who wore dowdy clothes. Satisfied? Let's go shopping."

"No, Mom. Not the TV show, the birds and the bees!"

"Okay, birds lay eggs and chicks are born. The male bee 'pollinates' the queen and then dies, which is how it should be. Get in the car."

I knew she was avoiding the topic and giving me fake answers (lies) to my question, but I refused to get up from my chair. As a child, I was nothing if not tenacious. As Chelsea Clinton recently wrote of her mother, *She Persisted.*

"Mom, I need to know how babies are made, and I'm not getting up from this chair until you tell me!"

"Melissa, if you don't get up from that chair, you'll never have babies. Why do you need to know? Is one of your classmates having a baby? I'll bet it's that Murphy girl, isn't it? What's her name...Susie...Sandy...Slutty. I never liked that family. Never trusted them. Especially the father. Always wears velour, even in the summer. Who does that? I'll bet they're drinkers too. You notice their lights are always off and sometimes the car is parked on the lawn? I heard they were the inspiration for *Who's Afraid of Virginia Woolf?*"

"First of all, Mom, her name is Denise. Second, she's not slutty. Third, the car was on the lawn because they were having the driveway repaved. And four...I can't explain the velour thing, either.

"Mom, I'm getting older, I need to know."

"Oh, alright. Let's go into the kitchen; we'll talk."

We went into the kitchen, where Betty was waxing the floor, cleaning the oven, relining the shelves, and polishing the semi-good silver.

"Betty, can I have an iced coffee? Missy, milk? Soda? A clever little Chardonnay, 1958, from the Loire Valley?"

We sat down at the table and Betty brought us our drinks.

"Hey, Mom, I didn't know coffee came in a bottle with a cork."

"Yes, Melissa," my mother said as she gulped down her "coffee." "Babies come from love. When a man and woman fall in love with each other, they have babies."

"Can two women have babies?"

"Yes, but they always fight over who's mommy number one."

"Can two men have babies?"

"Yes, Melissa. And they're always dressed impeccably. Do you remember the Reed–Jones boys from pre-school? The only toddlers who had seasonal wardrobes?"

"Can *all* men and women have babies?"

"No, sweetheart. Some couples can't have babies because either the man or woman has physical issues, or because the man is gay and only married a woman so his mother would stop asking him why he was forty-seven years old, rich, handsome, successful, still single, and why he had a college-aged roommate named Rusty."

"How will I know if I'm in love?"

"Oh, you'll know. You may date lots of boys, but one day, you'll meet Mr. Right. Not like your slutty friend, Denise, who'll meet Mr. Right Now. You'll feel a tingle in your hands and a pounding in your chest and you'll know right away that you're either in love or having a stroke. And when the pounding stops, if you're still able to walk, sit up, and talk without drooling, you'll know it's love. You'll take one look at him and think, 'Is this the man I'm going to someday have children with? Is this the man I'm going to someday fleece in court and take every fucking dollar he has?' If the answer to both those questions is 'yes,' then he's the one."

"Did that happen with you and Daddy?"

"Yes, Melissa, it did. It was love at first sight, especially for your father. I was a dog, but he had glaucoma. We were a perfect match."

"And you and Daddy loved each other?"

After a pause, she continued, "Okay, fine, yeah. Whatever. We made you, didn't we? So nosy."

"But how did you and Daddy *physically* make me?"

Exasperated with my inquisitiveness, she said, "Oh, for God's sake, Melissa. You're wearing me out."

My mother got up, ran into the den, grabbed a book from the bookcase, ran back into the kitchen, and plunked the book down in front of me. As she grabbed her giant mug of "coffee," and headed upstairs, she said, "Read this book, Melissa. It will tell you ALL you need to know about ALL the facts of life. Take notes, make copies, use a highlighter, I don't care. And when you're all done, if you still have questions, come and ask me."

The book was *The Happy Hooker*. And my mother was right. It answered all my questions.

Like a Virgin

I was sixteen when Madonna's "Like a Virgin" was released and became a huge, monster hit. I remember watching the video on MTV with my mother. When the song finished, my mother got up from the couch and said, "Madonna was never like a virgin, not even at birth. When she was born, she looked up at the obstetrician and said, 'Was it good for you?'" (Truth be told, my mom liked Madonna because Madonna ignored the critics and naysayers and built a great career by doing what she does, *her* way, and being true to herself.)

I think the most important conversation a mother can have with her daughter is the one that involves love, sex, virginity, and self-respect. Unless, of course, that mother was *my* mother, in which case the most important conversation involved residuals, royalties, award shows, and why "your father doesn't touch me anymore."

Most parents have the sex conversations with their children when the kid is around eleven or twelve. It's much earlier in Beverly Hills because the kids there are so much more "advanced." In Beverly Hills, a fourth grader is less likely to be driven to school by her daddy than by her baby-daddy. Or her attorney.

I don't remember the exact date that my mother finally did have the "virginity talk" with me, but I was, as she put it, "at the age where I could still attract a pretty penny on the black market."

"Melissa, I want to talk to you about sex; sit down."

"Mom, we're in Bergdorf's."

"Exactly! Bergdorf's is the perfect place for a sex talk, because if you're not well-dressed, no decent, successful, God-willing Jewish man will want to fuck you.

"Let's walk over to the plus-size section, where we can sit down. I've always hated the term 'plus-size.' It's ridiculous. Why not just say, 'Chubbo-I'm-Not-at-My-Goal-Weight Clothes'? That's what they are, clothes for girls who are still counting points."

"Mom, I'm not a marketing expert, but I'm pretty sure that calling them 'clothes above my goal weight' wouldn't be good for sales. Plus-size softens up the weight issue a bit."

"Well, in that case, why not call it the 'Have You Thought about a Salad?' section, or the 'Thank God She has a Good Personality' section?

"I feel the same way about junior petites or, even worse, size zero. How can anyone be a size zero? I know dead women who are at least a two. If a woman is a size zero, chances are, she's got either cancer or bulimia."

"Did you ever think maybe she's just thin?"

"Melissa, no one's that thin. Ethiopians live on sand and dust and even they can pull off a spaghetti strap without looking sickly.

"Oooh oooh, I just had a brilliant idea! Considering that all the size zeros have cancer or bulimia, I think Bergdorf's should sell the size zero dresses as a combo, Comes-with-a Fashionable-Purge-Pail. Think of the marketing slogans: 'Dress Up to Throw Up!' or, 'Hurl, Girl!' Ahhh..."

My mother's eyes glazed over, yet even through the opaque stare, I could see the wheels turning inside her head. In retrospect, I believe this was the exact moment in time when she had the idea to create her own fashion collection...an idea that came to fruition on QVC, and is still going strong today. All I'm saying is that a great idea came out of an ill-informed lie. Thanks to the Joan Rivers Collection, millions of women and gay men look fabulous in affordable clothes, scarves, accessories, and bee pins. And, in my mother's commitment to rigorous semi-honesty, the collection features clothes for plus-size, junior-petite, and size-zero women (and size half for the very lithe gay man).

So, we sat down in a couple of chairs to talk.

Back to sex...

"Your first time should be special; it should matter. Look, we've all given blow jobs to sailors during Fleet Week—"

"I haven't."

"—but doing *it* for the first time is important because there's only a first time once...for everything. Unless, of course, you're Shirley MacLaine, who's had three hundred different lifetimes. Can you imagine losing your virginity three hundred times? That's a lot of laundry to do.

"The most important thing you need to know is that the first time might be painful. And you might bleed a little. It's just like shaving your legs, except you don't have to worry about the razor's feelings or ego. And because it's your first time, you're under no pressure to be 'good in bed.' The man, however, is. You're supposed to be a virgin, he's not."

Before I could jump in with the obvious question, my mother continued on, answering it as if she could read my mind.

"I know, I know...how are men supposed to be experienced at sex if women are supposed to be virgins? Again, a no-brainer; that's why God invented sheep. I know, I know...there are no sheep in Manhattan, so how does that work out? Simple: didn't you ever wonder how we're able to buy lush, imported Angora sweaters downtown, at well below wholesale prices? Well, now you know; you're welcome.

"The other way men gain experience in sex is by going out with tramps. Believe it or not, *not* every girl is a virgin. You know all those 'Heidi Abramowitz was such a tramp' jokes I do in my act? They're all based on a girl I went to high school with. Her real name was...Heidi Abramowitz. She was like a gas station; every guy came in to 'fill 'er up.' I want your first time to be memorable. Candles, roses, soft lighting...like a casino lounge on Valentine's Day."

"Mom, do you remember your first time?"

"Like it was yesterday."

"When was it?"

"Yesterday."

"Mom?"

"About 4:00. The produce manager at Ralphs slipped me a quickie behind the lettuce stand."

"Seriously? You went to a supermarket? How stupid do you think I am?"

"Of course, I remember my first time, Melissa. I got a terrible headache; ruined the whole experience for me."

"What happened?"

"We were in the middle of doing it when the bathroom door cracked me in the head."

"MOM!"

"What? It wasn't my fault; the bus lurched."

"A bus? Your first time was on a city bus?!"

"Of course not; it was a Greyhound. What do you think I am?"

"Do you really want me to answer that? Forget that doing it in a bus bathroom is disgusting, wasn't it dangerous?"

"Yes! Especially because I was with the driver. You know Greyhound's slogan: 'Leave the Pile-Driving to Us!'"

That pause you hear is me trying to catch my breath. The thought of...well, you get it.

"My suggestion for your first time, Missy, is find a guy who's not too big. And by big, I don't mean tall or fat, I mean hung. You want to start out with a guy who's small, hung like a gerbil."

"How do you know how gerbils are hung?"

"Back in the day, I spent a drunken night with Richard Gere."

"That's so not true."

"Which part? The gerbil part or the I-slept-with-Richard-Gere part?"

"Both."

"Okay, I made it up. I don't even know Richard Gere; I'm sure he's lovely. And as for the gerbils, well, they're tiny; how hung could they be? Although, Sammy Davis, Jr. was tiny and he was packing some heat down there. Sammy only weighed a hundred pounds, but forty of it was shlong."

"You slept with Sammy Davis Jr.?"

"The only one bigger was Milton Berle's. Talk about *What Becomes a Legend Most*? Milton's had its own room at The Friars Club. If you ever heard someone say, 'Milton Berle, what a *putz*,' they meant it as a compliment.

"What I'm saying is, start small and work your way up. Let one of those tiny French acrobats from Cirque de Soleil open and Milton Berle close. Because if your first lover is someone like Milton, you'll get all stretched out and your vag will look like sheets blowing dry on a clothesline."

"Seriously? When is the last time you hung laundry on a clothesline?"

"Never. But I saw them do it once on *Little House on the Prairie*. Did you know that Michael Landon was Jewish? So was Lorne Greene, from *Bonanza*. Jewish settlers; how funny is that? Jews aren't known as settlers; we're known as lawyers who make settlements. Ah, I love irony."

"Mom, we should go. Those women over there are staring at us; I think they need the chairs."

My mother looked over, took a beat, and said, "Those aren't women, Melissa, they're woman. That's one person, she's just so big she looks like a group. Her name is Bertha and she lives around the corner from us. By the way, did you ever notice that all 'Berthas' are fat? It's true; you never see a skinny Bertha. It's the same way as 'Gertie' is an old lady's name. Seriously. All Gerties are old. When's the last time you saw Gertie in a crib?"

As we got up to leave, my mother cupped my face in her hands and gave me a kiss on the forehead.

"Sweetheart, I'm glad we had this talk. I hope it was helpful and I hope you learned something about losing your virginity."

"Actually, Mom, I did not."

"Why not?"

"Because I'm thirty-seven."

JOANS FAVORITE "HEIDI ABRAMOWITZ IS A TRAMP" JOKES

1. She doesn't have a G spot; she has the whole alphabet.

2. She keeps her birth control pills in a Pez dispenser.

3. Fast? Her bedspread is a checkered flag.

4. She is such a tramp, she's named in the acknowledgments of the *Kama Sutra*.

5. She never talks with her mouth full. She could hurt somebody.

6. I once asked her, "What do you do in bed?" She said, "About ten grand a year."

7. Heidi is really laid back, frequently.

8. That tramp. Her tongue gets Worker's Compensation.

9. She spends more time with her legs in the air than a dead cockroach.

10. Heidi gets a lot of exercise. Jumping Jacks, jumping Larrys, jumping Freds.

11. Her jeans are so tight, she has to have them fitted by a gynecologist.

12. She once got a job with a sperm bank but was fired for embezzling.

Driving Miss Crazy

I grew up in Los Angeles, which is known for its sunny climate, beautiful beaches, movie stars, and rehab clinics. But more than all that, it's known for its traffic. It's a city where it can take four hours to go eleven miles, and when someone asks, "How was your drive," you'll say, "Not bad." That's because *everyone* in LA has a car; some people have two or three cars. Jay Leno has 286 of them. Why does Jay have 286 cars? Beats me. Or as the Beach Boys would say, "God Only Knows." Who knows, maybe he's a hoarder? (My mother used to say, "Jay Leno will never be in a car accident, because his cars are like the punchlines in his act; you can see them coming from a mile away.")

Of course, in order to drive a car, you have to be able to drive. In California, you can get a driver's license at sixteen years of age...which means you have two years to run people over and still not be tried as an adult.

When I was fifteen, my mother taught me how to drive. Given that she was a terrible driver, it was, needless to say, a harrowing experience. The only thing that could have been more harrowing was if my father taught me to drive. My dad was British/South African, where they drive on the opposite side of the road than we do here in America. Whenever we'd be in the car going on a family outing with my dad behind the wheel, he had to resist switching lanes and driving into oncoming traffic. I can still hear my mother's constant refrains of "Edgar, stay on the right side of the road; we're in Brentwood, not Brighton."

I swear one time I heard him mumble, "I know."

To be fair, maybe I shouldn't have said my mother was a "terrible" driver; "inconsiderate" is a better descriptor (think Mr. Magoo in drag). She knew there were other cars on the road; she just chose not to pay attention to them. When my mother would drive on a freeway, there were so many horns honking at her, it sounded like an air raid siren warning the townsfolk about an impending attack.

The moment she got off the ramp and onto the freeway, it was like O.J.'s low-speed Bronco chase after he "allegedly" killed his ex-wife and her friend. One car, all by itself, ambling down the 405 with hundreds of cars trailing behind. The only differences were a) my mother didn't stab anyone and b) during the O.J. chase, all of the other cars were kept back by the police. In my mother's case, other drivers just didn't want to be anywhere the fuck near her. She was the coronavirus of drivers.

My mom taught me to drive forward, in reverse, turn left, turn right, and make U-turns—all without signaling; "Don't worry, it's a big car, they'll see me coming."

I remember the first time she took me to drive on a freeway. I was scared to death—six lanes of traffic in each direction, and the second I got off the entrance ramp, she insisted that I immediately merge all the way over to the far left lane. Once there, she kept saying, "Melissa, slow down, slow down, you're going too fast."

"Mom, I'm doing the speed limit," I said, "and isn't this the fast lane?"

"Slow down, lead foot," she yelled, even though I was barely doing sixty-five miles per hour.

Within two minutes, I had cars backed up behind me, jamming up the traffic flow, and had drivers honking their horns and giving me the finger.

"Why do you have me driving this slow in the passing lane? I'm going to cause an accident and kill someone!"

"Au contraire, Missy. You're actually saving lives. People in LA are always in such a rush, their stress level is through the roof; by slowing down the 'rushers' in the left lane, you're helping them by getting them to slow down and be in the moment. Less stress, less heart attacks. Namaste!"

Since I was so young, I sort of believed her—or, at the least, I was so nervous being on the freeway for the first time, I dared not argue lest I get completely rattled and drive off the road. In hindsight, I realize my mother wasn't telling the truth. She didn't want me driving slowly so I could save lives; she wanted me to drive slowly so we could have the road to ourselves, and she knew that if I fucked up the traffic flow, everyone would pass us, and we'd be all alone on the freeway. She wasn't being altruistic; she was being selfish. And lying.

The only thing my mother didn't teach me to do was park, because she didn't believe in it; she believed in valet parking. As a birthright.

"Melissa, everyone on the planet is here for a reason; God doesn't make mistakes. And men in short, red vests are meant to be parking valets. Or organ grinders, but when is the last time you saw a tiny monkey on the sidewalk, banging cymbals in 2/4 time? Who am I to deny parking attendants their destiny?"

"Mom, that's ridiculous. Not every place has valet parking. Remember the time you pulled into a Denny's parking lot and sat there for half an hour waiting for the valet to come park your car?"

"He came, didn't he?"

"He wasn't a valet, Mom, he was a cop. And he parked the car instead of having it towed only because you bribed him with tickets to your next show."

"Your point, Melissa?"

"My point is..."

"There is no point, Melissa. Valet parking—as well as other customer service jobs—began thousands of years ago. It's part of the human genetic code. When Noah got those animals on the Ark, do you think they just casually boarded, two by two, and knew exactly where to go, all by themselves? Of course not; there were valets and ushers to show them to their rooms. How else would giraffes know that the cabins with extra headroom were on the promenade deck if the valets didn't tell them? Have you ever seen kangaroos do anything in an orderly fashion, let alone sit in their assigned seats at the captain's table for dinner...especially at the first seating? No; there were ushers to make sure they hopped—quietly—to the appropriate chairs. And as for parking? Noah was too cheap to spend money for a parking attendant, and after the forty days of rain, what happened? *Shmuck* got stuck with a boatful of livestock on top of a mountain with nowhere to go, that's what happened. For eight bucks an hour plus tip, they would have floated all the way to Monaco for a fabulous weekend of tennis and grazing."

"Gee, Mom, do you have any examples that are maybe—oh, I don't know—a little more current? You know, from maybe the Iron Age or the Renaissance?"

"Do I? Remember the big funeral after the Kennedy Assassination? John Kennedy's funeral, not Bobby's; Bobby's was meh—way too many children—but JFK's funeral was an A-lister. Arlington Cemetery was packed, every seat was taken, and every shovel was spoken for. You know what Jackie did? Held her children's hands and grieved, stoically. You know what she didn't do? Park the hearse herself. She had *someone else* do it, probably a Secret Service guy she tipped a few bucks to make sure the casket didn't roll around in the back. Shall I go on? When Neil Armstrong became the first man to walk on the moon, did *he* park the Lunar Module? No, he and Buzz Aldrin got all gussied up and went for a stroll on the Sea of Tranquility and left poor Michael Collins alone in the capsule, circling the block, looking for a spot. And Neil and Buzz became national icons while Michael Collins became a *Jeopardy!* answer: Who is the loser who *didn't* walk on the moon because he was too busy parking? Want more?"

"No, no, no, you win; I don't need to learn to park."

Once again, as always, my mother wore me out. And, once again, as always, I foolishly believed her. For about a year after getting my license, no matter where I was going, when I got there, I just stopped my car in front of the place and left it, sitting unattended, waiting for a valet. After getting twenty-six parking tickets, having thirty-five nasty notes left on my windshield, and filing four stolen car claims with GEICO, it finally dawned on me that my mother was lying.

So, over her objections (and expressions of disappointment), I hired a driving instructor and learned to park...and I learned to park well. And if you don't believe me, ask the nine people whose bumpers I ever-so-slightly demolished in the parking lot of Trader Joe's.

Bad Hair Day

If nothing else, my mother was consistent. Since I was a young girl, no matter how I did my hair, it was wrong. If I wore it up, it should be down; if I wore it long, it should be short; if I wore braids atop my head, she'd ask me if my name was Gerta and where my *dirndl* was. (At least she stopped putting her finger over her lip and saying, "Heil Hitler," after she was kicked out of my third-grade production of *The Sound of Music*.) But the one thing she hated more than anything was when I had bangs. I can't count the number of times I'd walk into the kitchen with newly cut bangs, and she'd say, "Oh hi, Moe," as is in Moe, from The Three Stooges. Nice, huh? Nothing is better for a teenage girl's ego than being compared to a dead vaudeville comic who eventually gained television fame by poking his brothers in the eyes.

Through the years, I learned to counterpunch. So, every time she hit me with "Hi, Moe," I immediately shouted out the name of a famous woman who wore bangs:

"Hi, Moe."

"Bettie Page."

"Dead."

"Hi, Moe."

"Louise Brooks."

"Dead."

"Hi, Moe."

"Veronica Lake."

"Dead. And only had one bang."

"Hi, Moe."

"Cleopatra."

"Died single. And alone. Which is my fear for you, Melissa,
  if you insist on keeping those fucking bangs."

Finally, after years of this contentious bangs war I asked her why she was so obsessed with bangs. My mother's explanation, steeped in false history, explained a lot.

"Melissa, a woman's hair is the fourth thing a man notices—unless it's on her face, in which case it moves up to number three. Remember Frida Kahlo? World famous artist, but when you mention her name, what is the first thing anyone thinks about? Her giant unibrow, which was thicker and deeper than the Amazon rain forest. When I first saw a picture of her, I half expected Jane Goodall to come crawling out of her brow holding a chimpanzee peeling a banana. Most men find that sort of facial hair on a woman repulsive, but apparently Diego Rivera didn't. He loved Frida's brows so much, he called them his 'Field of Dreams.' Little known fact, Melissa: Diego Rivera came from a long line of electrolysis professionals. Some say his love for Frida was the ultimate rebellion; broke his mother's heart.

"But American men are different—while they don't like females with face fuzz, they do love a woman with a gorgeous head of hair...properly styled! For men, hair is either a turn on or a turn off. Let's be honest—when is the last time you saw a single, straight guy in Manhattan cruising the streets on the prowl for women with thinning hair? Never, that's when!"

"Mom, when is the last time you saw a single, straight guy in Manhattan, at all?" Believe it or not, this question momentarily stopped her in her tracks.

After regaining her composure, my mother continued, "Melissa, you're missing the point. Men love women with great hair. Julia Roberts has six hundred teeth, but gorgeous hair, and men flock to her. Remember Eleanor Roosevelt? Hardly a looker. Did you know that the first time FDR saw Eleanor was at one of those 'feminist' rallies she liked to attend? After a rousing game of 'Duck, Duck, Lezzie,' she took a break; one of her gal pals playfully pulled one of Eleanor's hairpins out with her teeth and her luscious locks tumbled down. Story goes, FDR saw this and was instantly smitten. (Rumor has it he so loved her tresses, he would only make love to her doggie style. At least that's the excuse he used.) One of the great marriages in American history was all started because of good hair."

Thinking this was the end, I started to walk away. But no, apparently she had a big finish.

"And, of course, Marie Antoinette, last queen of France before the revolution? Remember her? Hmmm? People think she was beheaded for committing treason. But *non!*"

(Whenever my mother used a word from a foreign language, I knew that we were in trouble and it was time to sit down.) "Not true, Marie! M. A., as I like to call her, was known for her elaborate hairstyles. She was the Farrah Fawcett of her day. On July 14th, 1789, she went to Mr. Maurice of the Champs-Élysées for her weekly wash and set. While under the dryer, she told Mr. Maurice how she was in a bit of a funk because those pesky peasants surrounding Versailles were trampling the freshly sodded lawn and not curbing their dogs. Mr. Maurice suggested a new look to help lift her mood. An hour later, Marie came home with bangs. Louis, shocked but not wanting to hurt her feelings, called them 'different' and told her to take a deep breath and, 'Don't worry, they'll grow out.' Inconsolable, Marie began mumbling something about eating a piece of cake...and well, you know how that ended."

I stared at my mother in disbelief, not for the first—or last—time. Nonplussed, she continued, "So when I tell you that I don't like your hair or your bangs, I tell you out of love and concern...and out of the fact that I don't want to you to wind up either a dried-up spinster or a headless horsewoman. Understand? I criticize because I love you. Why is it so hard for you to understand that I am protecting you from yourself?"

Of course, I understood. I understood that my mother would lie through her teeth to get what she wanted...or in her words, "Because I love you."

My debutant ball. Why am is smiling? Because I haven't yet been told that I wasn't adopted.

Happy Holidays!

My mother loved holidays. I'm not sure if it was the giving or the receiving, but any time a major holiday was coming up, my mom would get so happy and sweet and excited, she practically became another person. Instead of worrying about work and becoming resentful of those people who were getting the jobs she felt she should have gotten, she'd think about buying those people gifts—like nooses or cyanide pills or cars with faulty brakes.

According to her, holidays are the main reason we're Jewish. "Melissa, there are like a gazillion religions in the world—Christianity, Islam, B'hai, Shintoism, Hinduism, Buddhism, Sikhism, Jainism, Animism—and they all have something good to offer.

"Take the Sikhs, for example. They wear turbans. Perfect religion if you're having a bad hair day. You should speak to one of them about how to wrap your hair if you're between colorings or your stylist is out of town at a pride parade. I realize there are not many people of that faith in our neighborhood, but my advice is Sikh and ye shall find."

"Mom, really?"

"Same as the Muslims. They're very big with the head coverings too. Like the Sikhs, they mostly live in hot, arid deserts where it's very hard to hold a perm or a curl, and split-ends are the norm. Those hijabs come in very handy in July and August."

"What about the burkas? They cover everything."

"Again, Melissa, it's about the hair. I heard that Muslim women are extremely hairy. Their legs get five o'clock shadow. But throw on a burka and, BOOM, just like that, smooth as a pageant winner.

"You know, all of this hair talk makes me realize that a lot of religions are very hat-oriented. And it's trending."

"Is that why our neighbor, Mr. Jones, started wearing a cap? Is he going B'hai?"

"No, B'hald. Mr. Jones is getting hair plugs, but they haven't grown in yet. He looks like that Barbie doll you had when you were six. Remember? You got mad at me for making you cut your bangs, so you shaved Barbie's head in protest. It was so embarrassing. I didn't want to tell people you were being bratty, so I said that Barbie had alopecia, like Mike Nichols, and we were going to bring her to a doll hospital for experimental treatments. Actually, it turned out very well. Rather than have them think I must be a lousy mother to have driven you to disfigure your doll, they'd say, 'Mike Nichols has alopecia? Does his wife, Diane Sawyer, know?'

"I'd say, 'Does she know? She loves it!' Mike has no body hair whatsoever. When Mike gets out of the bathtub, he looks like a giant toddler or Baby Huey.

"One time I was at a girls' lunch with Barbara Walters, Joy Behar, Whoopi Goldberg, and Diane. The food comes and Diane yells out, 'Omigod, there's a hair in my soup! Where did it come from?'

"I said, 'Not Mike Nichols.' Everyone laughed and laughed. Except Diane."

"Is that why Diane hasn't spoken to you in years?"

"Who knows? I'm sure she has plenty of other reasons. You know who really loves hats? The pope. The man is obsessed; he's the Imelda Marcos of millinery. He has an entire floor of the Vatican devoted entirely to his hat collection. Just like Elton John has for his wiglets."

"Elton John has a floor at The Vatican?"

"Of course not, Melissa, I'm making an analogy. This explains your SAT verbal scores. Elton's not Catholic. I've heard that Elton refers to his wigs as 'the girls.' How fabulous is that? They all have names. One is Maxine, one is Jennifer, one is Michaela, and so on. He wears a different girl for each concert. Except for Fridays; he always wears Miriam on Fridays, you know, to honor the Sabbath."

My mother must have noticed my look of incredulity (I was rolling my eyes so much I made myself dizzy), so she shifted gears.

"Oh...the pope. Remind me to come back to the Sabbath. So, the pope is quite the hat aficionado. You know, if he wasn't the pope, I'd think he was just a very pious hoarder. Most often we see him with a beanie, but every now and again, depending on his mood, he'll throw on a nifty fez or a sassy little cloche. He says they're fun to accessorize."

"Really, Mom? When did he say that?"

"A few years ago. He told me. We wound up sitting together at the theater."

"Theater?"

"On Broadway. We were seeing *Agnes of God*. Do you know he knew all the words and sang along to every song?"

"Mom! *Agnes of God* is *not* a musical."

"Well, he was moving his lips during the entire show. Maybe he was praying, or maybe he was just muttering to himself about the woman sitting in front of us with the huge bouffant that was blocking our view. She must have been from Jersey."

"And in the middle of the play, you just leaned over and said, 'Excuse me, Pope, what's your favorite hat?'"

"Of course not. What's that matter with you? First off, I called him Your Eminence, and second, it was during inter-mission. He was in line for the men's room. Apparently, that Blood of Christ really runs through ya. I offered him a Kit Kat and said, 'I love your Beanie. It's like a yarmulke with a nipple.'

"He laughed and said, 'I hear that all the time. Mostly from the Jews. You'll never guess what my favorite hat is. G'head; try.'

"'Porkpie?'

"He laughed and said, 'Pork, ha-ha; again, the Jews! No, the miter. I love my miter.'

"'I love it too, Your Eminence. It's like a dunce cap with rubies!'

"'Oh my God, Joan, you kill me! I love it because it sits high and elongates my face. Gives me length and makes me look less stocky and stooped. So much cheaper than having work done.'

"'*Now*, you tell me. Where were you twenty years ago when I was having my chin done?'"

We went back to our seats and exchanged numbers. I was going to ask him if he wanted to go backstage and say "hi" to the cast with me, but he had to leave before the bows. Something about blessing orphans or bringing relief to famine victims, who the fuck knows? Anyway, he was quite lovely."

For what seemed like forever, I sat there and stared at her. Finally, my jaw unfroze, and I said, "Mom, do you expect me to believe that? That not only did you meet the pope in a Broadway theater, but that you remembered your entire conversation with him, verbatim?"

"Well of course I did, Melissa. I'm pretty sure if you were ever lucky enough to meet a pope, you'd remember every word too. He'd probably say, 'So nice to meet you, Melissa. What's up with the bangs?'"

"Really? You think the pope would take time out of his busy day to comment on my bangs?"

"If he has time to go hat shopping, he has time for your bangs."

"Fine. Here's your reminder: Sabbath."

"Ooohhh, thank you sweetheart. I love you. Even with your bangs. You know, it's not really about the Sabbath; it's about why we're Jewish."

"I'm guessing because Grandma and Grandpa were Jewish?"

"No, but good guess. It's because the Jewish religion has lots of holidays, that's why. Think about it—everyone gets off from work or school on Christian holidays, like Christmas or Easter, so it's no big deal. It's the same as national holidays, like the Fourth of July or Presidents' Day or Columbus Day. Everyone is off. But Jews get a lot of *extra* days off because we have so many holidays: Rosh Hashanah, Yom Kippur, Purim, Tisha B'Av, Chanukah, and Passover. Put all those holidays together and we've got at least a month's free paid vacation! And because nobody ever questions the validity of a religious holiday, we can make even the flimsiest of holidays into a 'day of remembrance,' or some other bullshit.

"Don't scowl at me, Melissa..."

"I'm not scowling at you."

"But you were going to. I know you; I'm your mother. I gave birth to you. Or so I'm told.

"I wasn't finished what I was saying when you began scowling. And if you don't stop scowling, I'm not going to finish. I think most Jewish holidays are really, really good, especially if I can celebrate them without having to go to synagogue. Anytime a major holiday rolls around, and I already have important plans for that day, like washing the feet of the poor, or curing cancer, or shopping, I always tell the rabbi I can't make it because I have a sinus infection and he never quibbles, because a) name one Jew who doesn't have a sinus infection and b) I've had so many nose jobs, he's happy I still have sinuses."

For those of you reading this who are not Jewish, not familiar with our holidays, or live in Iowa, most of our holidays are similar to yours: Rosh Hashanah is the Jewish New Year, and we celebrate it like a regular New Year with lots of food and lots of fun. The only difference is, we don't hang around Times Square getting drunk or flashing our tits while waiting for a ball to drop.

Purim is the story of Mordecai, Haman, Queen Esther, and evil King Ahasuerus. I know what you're thinking: sounds more like a reality show on BET than a Bible story. I concur.

A week or so after Rosh Hashanah is Yom Kippur, our annual day of atonement. We observe this holiday by fasting for twenty-four hours to atone for our sins. We break the fast with lots of food, most of it very high in fats, carbohydrates, and starch. Which explains why it took us forty years to cross the desert. Jewish food is so heavy, we had to stop every half mile to rest or look for a bathroom or buy some ex-lax.

Which brings me to Passover, which was my mother's favorite Jewish holiday (mostly because it lasts for a week and she could milk extra days off from whatever it was she was being paid to do). Passover is the story of the Jews' exodus from Egypt, which is chronicled in Book 1 of the Bible, "Exodus."

At our last Passover together, my mother thought we could make a new cable TV movie of the story and change the title from Exodus to *Fifty Shades of Schlepping*.

The main part of Passover is the Seder, in which family and friends from all over gather and have a huge dinner that includes songs and prayers and the telling of the story of the exodus. It's like a Christmas dinner without presents, ham, or Jesus. My mother hosted Passover Seders every year, and it became an annual tradition, like the Running of the Bulls in Pamplona.

One of the highlights of the Seder is the Four Questions, which is the CliffsNotes version of the history of Passover (not to be confused with the self-help book, *The Four Agreements*, because Jews don't do self-help; we do expensive therapists, who not only walk us through our anxieties and problems, but also serve as nifty tax write-offs). The Four Questions are always asked by the youngest child at the table, and answered by one of the wisest, most sage adults. One memorable year, with about thirty people at the Seder, I was the youngest one there, so I asked the Four Questions. And my mother, who liked to be referred to as The Oracle of Bel Air, answered them. Not truthfully, of course.

"Okay, question one: Why is this night different than all other nights? And why do we dip twice?"

"Well, Melissa, it's different because your Aunt Barbara isn't here, and she usually is—I think she hurt her back power-shopping at Neiman Marcus. That's what you get from doing cardio. And we dip twice because it makes dancing more fun. Okay, next question."

"Why on this night do we eat only unleavened bread?"

"According to the Haggadah, it's because the Pharaoh's soldiers were coming to kill all the Jews, so we had to take our breads out of the oven before they were done. We wound up with matzah, which is, quite frankly, tasteless, unless it has caviar on it. That story is such BS. When is the last time you saw a Jewish woman hunched over an oven, baking? Never, that's when. That's why God invented Saltines."

"I know this isn't one of the questions, but why did the Pharaoh want to kill the Jews? What did we do?"

"*We* didn't do anything, Melissa; your great-great-great-great-great-great-uncle Elliott, did. There was no one specific thing Elliott did, he was just unbelievably annoying. All the time. He was whiny, he was twitchy, he chewed with his mouth open, and he had BO and dandruff. Even the other Jews wanted to kill him. Next!"

"Okay, question number three: Why on this night do we eat bitter herbs?"

"Melissa, I work in Hollywood. Bitter is my middle name. Time for question four; go!"

"Okay, why on this night do we eat while reclining instead of sitting up?"

"Melissa, have you ever had post-partum depression?"

"Mom, I'm eleven."

"When a woman gets depressed, particularly after she gives birth…to a baby she loves, even though the baby has ruined her figure and stretched her vagina so wide Chilean miners could get stranded in it, she often gets depressed. And she lies down in bed, flat on her back, and eats nothing but Fritos, ice cream, and Klonopin until she feels better. Six months later, when she finally gets up and looks in the mirror, she is so repulsed by what she sees, she gets back in bed.

"As for the men, they eat while reclining because the food is so binding, they can't get up. Did you know that one year, your Uncle Allan ate so much matzah he didn't shit until October? True story. I hope that answers all the questions!"

The other twenty-eight people at the table sat there aghast, with their mouths open, like that scene from *The Producers* where the audience is horrified watching the musical number, "Springtime for Hitler."

My mother didn't notice. She put down her Haggadah and said, "Dessert, anyone?"

In hindsight, I think another reason my mother loved Passover is that since she was hosting—it was her house, her food, her Seder—she could lie with impunity and never get called out on it.

L'chaim!

PS: One year my mother had a Passover Seder for all of her gay friends. It was so much fun. Two of the Four Questions involved Liza Minnelli.

PPS: If you want the real answers to the Four Questions, Google "Passover."

PPPS: Imagine my surprise when the pope showed up at our house that year for Thanksgiving.

Chanukah at the Rosenberg house. Please note the Jewish star hanging on the tree. My mother's version of Middle East Peace.

"Mom, we're Jewish; why do we have a Christmas tree?"

"Because you can't fit really big presents under a menorah; that's why, Melissa."

You Light Up My Life

One of my earliest memories of my mother "playing with facts" happened around Christmastime, when I was in first or second grade. It was early evening, and we were walking the dog (and by "we were walking the dog," I mean our housekeeper was walking the dog—a mastiff named Tiny—and we were walking behind her, holding hands, with my mom saying things like, "Tiny, don't pull so hard; you'll hurt Betty and she hasn't cleaned the kitchen yet."), when suddenly all of the Christmas lights in the neighborhood began going on. I loved it. I asked, "Mom, why don't we get to celebrate Christmas?" She replied, "Because we killed Jesus, dear, that's why.

"Christmas, shmistmas; if Jews did celebrate Christmas, it would be much nicer. For starters, the bulbs wouldn't be red and green, they'd be a soft pink, which makes everyone look ten years younger. Secondly, there wouldn't be reindeer on the roof. How would they get down? Do I need to remind you of the time that possum family got into our attic?

"Next...manger?... Really? I mean honestly, what Jew lives like that? It would be like us living in our cabana at the beach club, except with no air conditioning, lounge chairs, or a pool boy named Ronaldo."

"What about the three wise men?"

"Men, yes, wise, not so much. Schlepping to Sedona is one thing; schlepping to a manger in the middle of a barren desert is another. Why did they schlep to a manger in the middle of the desert? And clearly none were gay, because no one mentioned that they could turn the manger into a cute, three-bedroom, mid-century modern they could flip in six months." (May I remind you that I was about six when we had this "conversation" about real estate and potential investment properties.) "And by the way," she continued, "three men, alone, on a road, and not one of them is even a little bi-curious. Odd?"

As we walked past a house with what seemed like a million Christmas lights on it, I naively asked, "Mom, who discovered electricity?"

"Benjamin Franklin."

"Was he Jewish?"

"Does 'Benjamin Franklin' sound Jewish? No, Melissa, in fact he was so not Jewish, his wife had a foreskin. But he was brilliant. He was like a fat Bill Nye the Science Guy. Ben even proved that lightning was electricity. He tied a key to a kite and went out to fly the kite in the rain. Sure enough, there were bolts of lightning that hit the key and sent an electrical current all the way into Ben's fingers. As the rain came down, providing nourishment for the flowers and trees, Ben stood there, soaking wet, his arms and hands burnt to a crisp.

"But did that stop him? Noooo! As soon as his limbs stopped smoldering, he ran into the house and began writing his most famous book, *Poor Richard's Almanack*. But since Ben had no hands left, he had to write the entire manuscript using a crayon between his toes and a pair of charred stumps. And in less time than you can say, "Next time make sure you ground yourself," Ben had accidentally invented charcoal! The man was a genius.

"He immediately patented charcoal, much to the delight of court-room sketch artists, barbecue aficionados, and his bank account. Which is why *his* face is on the hundred-dollar bill and Lincoln's is only on the five. Freeing the slaves was good, but inventing electric current was profitable."

As we got to our front door, I asked, "Mom, is any of that true?"

"Missy," she said, "would I lie to you?"

Then she turned back, looked down the sidewalk and called out to Betty, who had fallen behind us due to the rotator cuff injuries she'd suffered on the walk, "Step on it, Betty. Those dishes aren't going to wash themselves!"

And to all a good night.

The Garden of Eden

I was an "inquisitive" child...always snooping around, asking questions, trying to figure out what was going on in the world and why. There was nothing I didn't want to know. When I asked my mother how the earth came to be, she told me there were two schools of thought—one was called evolution and the other, creationism. When I asked her which was accurate, she said, "Neither. And both.

"Melissa, the world *wasn't* created in seven days, but seven *business* days. And it wasn't just a couple of molecules forcibly colliding in the CERN particle accelerator. Honestly, it was all a completely avoidable accident, born out of neglect and shoddy workmanship."

According to her, on the fifth day, at the end of the shift, there was some sort of an electrical "issue." Since this "issue" was discovered after hours (not that anything was being done without a permit), the only person willing to come out and fix it was going to charge time and half, and since God was Jewish...well, anyway, there was an explosion on Sunday morning...

"...which, Melissa, we now refer to as the Big Bang, not to be confused with the noxious explosion Gandhi let out after his first bowl of curry after years and years of fasting. Remind me to tell you later about the elephant whose eyebrows got singed.

"Little known fact: Big Bang is what my orthodox friends call Lot's wife. Did you know that Lot's wife was never actually given a name in the Bible? She's just referred to as 'Lot's wife,' as though she's not worth naming. (Sure, Disney came up with names for all seven dwarfs, but not one person in the Bible could come up with a name for that poor woman? No wonder she had insecurities. Pretty disrespectful, I'd say, especially when you consider that Mrs. Lot was the first person *ever* to be turned into a pillar of salt, which is kind of a big accomplishment. It also gave rise to centuries of wealthy, Jewish cardiologists with full hospital privileges."

(Today, there is actually a monument called "The Pillar of Salt"—nee Lot's wife—at the edge of the Dead Sea, just outside of Sodom.[3] According to my mother, it's right next to the Pillar of Pepper, which was said to be built in honor of Mrs. Lot's effeminate BFF, Leon, who was known all over the land for his biting wit and sarcastic nature, not to mention an incredible flair with light yet durable fabrics. But I digress.)

Anyway, cut to Monday morning, eight-*ish*, Starbucks on Garden of Eden Drive South (the one in the good

---

[3] Anyway, lest she be thought of as a Sodomite, Lot's wife fled Sodom, and settled a hundred miles away, in Sodom adjacent. Why she didn't just go to Gomorrah, Sodom's sister city (they were the Minneapolis-St. Paul of their day), which was just down the road, I'll never know. The only thing Gomorrah was known for was a large, non-union hat factory and a CVS with twenty-four-hour pharmacy.

neighborhood). Adam and Eve leave with their venti lattes (soy milk for Adam; many people don't know this, but lactose intolerance was already a thing), arguing over whose fault the explosion was and who was going to have to take one for the team and tell the boss, G-Money (you know who I'm talking about, *Him*, the brother on high).

"So, Eve pulled out her Blackberry ('Yes, Melissa, a Blackberry—stop rolling your eyes at me!') and called the insurance company to put in a claim. Eve said the contractor they found on Craigslist wasn't bonded. The agent replied, 'Well, why didn't you check them out on Yelp or Angie's List? What kind of a moron are you?' Eve, always the first one to throw someone under the bus, said, 'Don't blame me; it wasn't my choice to hire Adam's idiot brother-in-law. Adam told me he was the guy who built Noah's giant zoo boat. How bad could he be?'"

At this point in the story, my mother took the opportunity to impart some "wisdom" to me. "Melissa, now you know understand why I'm not investing in your third cousin Leonard's theme restaurant, a culinary tribute to the Potato Famine. My gut says it's just not gonna work. And as for Adam and Eve, they lost the claim, they lost the house, they lost Eden. And Leonard's going to lose his shirt."

PS: Am I the only one who finds it weird that Adam and Eve were both brother and sister, and husband and wife? And that no one at TLC ever reached out to give them a show?

"Melissa! Jesus wasn't the only Jew who could walk on water!"
(Any photos showing my mother's arms are harder to find than
Jimmy Hoffa.)

Wedding Bell Blues

John and I got married on December 12, 1998. It was a big, New York City wedding. Not big like in 1982 when Rev. Sun Myung Moon married two thousand people at the same time in Madison Square Garden, but big by non-cult-member standards. (I was amazed that two thousand couples got married en masse; my mother was amazed that two thousand couples wore the exact same outfits.) John and I had about 350 guests. It was held at The Plaza Hotel, not just because the hotel was iconic—think final scene of *The Way We Were* with Barbra Streisand and Robert Redford—but because it was around the corner from my mother's house, and she could run back and forth bringing the wedding gifts home for safekeeping. ("Melissa, when is the last time a coat check girl *didn't* steal something?") We had a gorgeous Winter Wonderland-Dr. Zhivago theme. All that was missing were a couple of frozen Russian soldiers and Omar Sharif.

Truth be told, John and I would have been happy with a small wedding in California, where we both lived. We thought maybe fifty or sixty guests, a rabbi and pastor, and a very LA location—maybe the beach in Venice, or a cliff side in Malibu, or the parking lot of the Scientology Center. The rabbi and the pastor were the only things from that list that became a reality. Why, you ask? Because my mother made us an offer we couldn't refuse, that's why. (Yes, I'm aware of *The Godfather* reference.) If we did as we wanted and held the wedding in LA, I would have to do all of the planning on my own; if we decided to hold the wedding in New York, as my mother wanted it, she would be able to "help" me, her skills at emotional blackmail on full display. Since the thought of planning a wedding was as overwhelming as listening to "Yoko Ono Live," and a year of listening to my mother say, "That's not the way I would have done it," the choice seemed like a no-brainer; in a New York minute, I said, "Yes! New York!" Turns out the choice *was* a no-brainer...and I was the one with no brain. You would think by now I could speak "Joan" fluently, but you'd be wrong. Apparently, we had very different definitions of the word "help."

When one thinks of the word "help," you might think of the Beatles' song/movie, or the film, *The Help*, where Octavia Spencer gives her horrible boss a shit pie for dessert. To my mother, the offer of "let me help" and "opportunity to dominate and control" are synonymous, and my wedding turned out to be the perfect example of *her* definition of help.

The first bit of "help" came with picking the New York City location. Since John and I were both nature lovers (we met through our love of horses; I rode competitively and he was a trainer and owner), we thought something outdoors (with an indoor backup plan, of course) would be appropriate, like Central Park, the Statue of Liberty, or Rockefeller

Center. My mother picked The Plaza. "Melissa, there are steps to get into the building, not to mention a curb. That's more than outdoorsy enough!"

"Mom, John and I love being outdoors, under the stars, being one with nature."

"First of all, you and John would be two with nature, not one. I know math wasn't your best subject, but for fuck's sake, one and one is two. Or, as I think of it, invitee plus one. And secondly, you know who spends a lot of time outdoors, under the stars? The homeless, that's who. When you and John are walking down the aisle, do you want to have to step over Filthy Phil, the hobo from Cleveland with the lazy eye and fingernails like Howard Hughes?"

"No, of course, no...wait a minute. You actually know this homeless person? You have your own bum? How do you know him?"

"We had a thing, Melissa. Brief, but very intense."

"You had a 'thing' with a homeless man?"

"No one likes judgey, Melissa. FYI, there's something very sexy about an old, white man with hard, black feet."

I took a long pause, the kind of pause a death row prisoner takes while waiting for the governor to call. "Okay, I'll play along. So, Mom; how did you and Phil meet? Tinder? eHarmony? A Homeless Without Partners meeting?"

"Nope. One day, Margie Stern and I were having lunch at Le Cirque. When we left the restaurant, we went our separate ways. Margie got in a cab to go home, and I went to the alley around back to berate the busboy who put ice in my drink after I specifically asked for no ice. And what do I see? A homeless man, digging through the garbage hopper, looking for discards and leftovers. I thought, 'Repulsive, but smart!'

"Those were the same, exact qualities that first drew me to Stephen Hawking. Ahh, I remember that naughty weekend Stevie and I spent in Brighton like it was yesterday. The two of us on the rocky beach, watching the waves crash against the pebbles and stones. I can still feel the gentle wind at my back as I walked back up the beach to our hotel, yelling over my shoulder to Stephen, 'Jesus Christ, doesn't that thing go any faster? We have dinner reservations at 8:00!' Yes, Melissa it was a simpler and more carefree time.

"Anyway, back to Phil. Did you know there are almost twenty-five thousand restaurants in Manhattan? He could dumpster dive at any one of them, but no! He's smart enough to pick the finest, five-star restaurant in the entire city. The entire country! He's not scrounging for burritos in the trash bin at Taco Bell or rummaging through the refuse at KFC looking for chicken bones or coleslaw. No! he's treating himself to caviar and chateaubriand and chocolate mousse. My kind of man."

"You slept with Stephen Hawking?"

"Yes, Melissa. And we did way more than sleep. Two words: Sponge. Baths. I'll give you more of the dirty details about my fling with Studly Steve another time."

I agreed to having the wedding at The Plaza before my mother had a chance to share any more inappropriate-to-tell-a-stranger-let-alone-your-daughter information with me.

Lest you think I'm a spoiled ingrate, let's be clear, I'm not complaining, just informing. The Plaza Hotel is fabulous.

Michael Douglas and Catherine Zeta-Jones got married there. (I wonder if her mother "helped" her?) Lots of celebrities actually lived there: Cecil Beaton, Marlene Dietrich, Christian Dior, F. Scott Fitzgerald and his allergy-riddled wife, F. Snot Fitzgerald (sorry, just made me giggle), and, as my mother would say, "That little bitch Eloise. How does she get to have the run of the hotel? Her mother must be sleeping with the manager."

The Plaza is so fabulous that the bridesmaids could wear the ugliest dresses ever and still look good. Okay, maybe not good, but passable. Which wasn't an issue for *us* at *our* wedding because *my* mother picked out *their* dresses. She also "helped" me with my wedding dress, which was designed by Vera Wang. I don't mean the Vera Wang label; I mean Vera Wang. Herself. *The* Vera Wang.

For a (first-time) bride, having Vera Wang custom design your wedding dress is a big friggin' deal. It's like getting your first tongue kiss from Gene Simmons. It can be overwhelming. But after the first few minutes at my initial fitting, something became quite evident to me: my participation had been downgraded to dress mannequin with a pulse. For example, the sketches I had approved looked absolutely nothing like what I was trying on. Apparently, my mother and Vera had had a session about me, without me. "Oh, don't be ridiculous; who are you to question Vera Wang's creativity? I made a few suggestions, that was it."

My mother and Vera would talk as if I wasn't even there, the way people talk about damp, dementia-riddled, drooling Grandpa, while he's sitting in the corner of the den, not five feet away from them. Vera and my mom would occasionally ask me questions about something I wanted and then roll their eyes at me. Every now and then, I'd engage them in a brief debate about the dress. Guess who won those debates? Here's a clue: not me. If my mother had wanted me in a suit of armor instead of a dress, I'd have been clanging and banging my way down the aisle. It would have been *Love Story* meets *Game of Thrones*.

My mother didn't stop there. She had her "helping" hands all over the guest list too. The way it worked was, John and I had to make up a list of the people we wanted to invite and submit it to my mother. Imagine how shocked I was when our list came back with revisions and notes. It was more like submitting a script to a network than a guest list to my mother. "You want to invite her? *Why*? She was mean to you in third grade! Unless she's dying of some tropical disease and you're in the will, this is not a good booking. Let's try for someone else, maybe someone with show biz connections or at least someone rich enough to buy you a really good gift."

My mother also provided "help" with the catering, the flowers, the gift bags, the valet parking, and the bathroom attendants. (One of my gay stylists says he loathes men's room attendants; HATESHATESHATES them. He once said, "Let me get this straight. I'm going to spend time in a public men's room and pay a guy to *not* touch my dick? I don't think so!" I see his point.)

Basically, there were very few wedding details my mother left under my control. I was allowed to pick the band from choices she submitted ("Really Mom, the Lennon Sisters?"), and I was allowed to join the food tasting and cake tasting. She narrowed everything down to where I got a choice...and the "choices" were always things she wanted. And she presented them in a fair and balanced way. ("I like *these* napkins, Melissa, not the ones you picked, but what do I know; I'm only known as one of the greatest hostesses of New York. But don't let me tell you what to do; it's your choice.")

I'm lucky I got to choose the groom. And even luckier my mother liked him. If not, she would have tried to arrange a marriage for me, like they did in the Jewish *shtetls* of Russia back in the day.

Anyway, the wedding was covered by all the media, from *People* magazine to the *New York Times*. Apparently, everyone had a lot of fun...or so I'm told. I wouldn't know. I was passed around like a collection plate on a Sunday, shuffled from one area to the next and from one guest to the next. I felt less like a bride than a nurse at a free clinic. At one point, I found myself alone, with no idea as to what I was supposed to do or where I was supposed to be. So, I did what any self-respecting bride would do...I went into the ladies' room to take a couple of deep breaths, check my makeup, rest my feet, and smoke one of the cigarettes I'd hidden in stall number four before the ceremony.

As the night wound down and John and I were going to head back to our room, I saw John's best man helping my mother load up her limo with centerpieces, flower arrangements, silverware, dishes, and anything else she could steal or fit into the trunk. I took her aside and said, "Mommy, first of all, I want to thank you for helping me plan this amazing wedding. I love you."

"Help you? What the fuck are you talking about? You didn't lift a finger; I had to do it all myself."

"And second, how did you get the best man to help you pilfer all this shit?"

"Easy. I offered him ten percent. And by the way, he isn't really the 'best man'; I've had plenty better."

"You slept with the best man?"

"That's a story for another day, my precious. I love you sweetheart; have a wonderful wedding night. And don't forget to moan like you're actually enjoying yourself."

With advice like that, is it any wonder the marriage didn't last? Although John and I couldn't make our marriage work long-term, we remain best friends and beautifully co-parent our spectacular son, Cooper. If it wasn't for John, there would be no Cooper. And if it wasn't for my father, my dad could've been Filthy Phil.

The Big, Bad Wolfs

I knew my mother was head-over-heels in love with Cooper the day he was born. Yes, she fawned over him and showered him with gifts and spoiled him rotten, as all grandmothers do, but it was more than that. She had some kind of connection to him. The only time I'd seen that before was in the movie *My Left Foot*. Daniel Day-Lewis's intense, loving relationship with the stairs he had to slither down was both deep and passionate. The way Daniel looked at that bannister...well, to this day, it still brings a tear to my eye.

The first time my mother saw Cooper was in my hospital room the day after he was born. She would have come right away, but she was performing at a Shriners' luncheon in Fresno and didn't want to give up the eight hundred bucks. (They were paying her in cash.)

"Mom, don't you want to know his name?"

"Okay."

"Mom, his name is Cooper. Isn't he beautiful?"

"Don't take this the wrong way, but no, he's not."

"Gee Mom, how could I possibly take that the wrong way?"

"What I meant was that the expression, 'all babies are beautiful,' is bullshit. Most babies aren't beautiful, certainly not when they come out. They're disgusting. They're gooey and slimy and purple. The only way you can tell them apart from the afterbirth is that the baby has eyes. Once they get rinsed off and cleaned up by the nurse, they start to look presentable. You know, if you think about it, the nurse is really just a baby's first stylist. The point is, Melissa, that prior to being born, babies spend months in cramped quarters that get even tighter as the weeks go by. It's like squeezing a size nine foot into a size six shoe. Eventually, when you take the shoes off, your feet are all banged up and bruised and swollen. It's not a pretty picture. It takes time for everything to settle. Don't you remember when you asked me, 'Am I pretty?' and I said, 'You will be'?"

"Of course, I remember that; I was thirteen; thirteen *years* old, not thirteen *minutes* old. That was such a mean thing to say."

"But was I wrong? No! You're beautiful! Well, maybe not at this exact moment. I mean, right now, you've still got the IV tubes and the drains in, and your eyes are all swollen from the grunting and pushing. I'm not even going to mention the amount of baby weight you've put on. Plus, you have that funky, nasty hospital smell, but like I said before, you will be beautiful again...as soon as those things are fixed."

In spite of my mother's contention that Cooper—and all babies—are hideous, she loved him more than anything... except buying bespoke jewelry at bargain basement prices.

When Cooper was an infant, immediately after his feeding, my mom would put him over her shoulder and burp him. And as soon as she felt a burp or a little baby-vomit coming up, she'd yell, "No, not on the Chanel!" and hold his head over Betty's lap so he could hurl on her and her store-bought apron. It was very touching, to say the least.

As Cooper got older, my mother was with him every step of the way. She helped teach him to walk even though she hoped he'd be rich enough that he didn't have to. She taught him his ABCs ("A is for Amex, V is for Visa"; it was like having Sue Grafton in the house), and she helped him with arithmetic by teaching him how to tip appropriately.

But my favorite thing was watching her read nursery rhymes and stories to him. After dinner, she'd curl up on the couch, knock back a coupla Jack and Cokes, sit Cooper in her lap, and tell him stories. I remember the first time vividly, because it did not go well.

"Melissa, before I get into actual stories, I want to make the kid smile and laugh, so I thought I'd tell him a little joke or recite a funny limerick or tongue-twister."

But before I could say, "no," she gave him a big squeeze and began. "Ok, Connor, here we go! 'There once was a man from Nantucket, whose di...'"

"Mom! Are you crazy? You can't tell him that one. It's filthy!"

"Oh, okay, sweetheart. Let me try this one. Are ya' ready, Carson? 'There once was a man named Schwartz, whose di...'"

"MOM! What is wrong with you?"

"I'm sorry, Missy. I played a Rotary Club Stag Mixer this afternoon and I'm still in 'show mode.' I brought a book, so I'll just read it to him."

"Fine."

The book was *Portnoy's Complaint* and it wasn't "fine." Like I said, the first time didn't go well. After that, I stayed in the room for the next few story time sessions and recorded everything in case Cooper and I might ever need to play them back for therapists, social workers, or our legal team.

So, she began reading.

"Hansel and Gretel were a brother and sister living with their parents in a house in Germany. Kind of like Donny and Marie with lederhosen. Times were tough. There was a food shortage, so the mother decided that the children ate too much and since there wasn't enough food for everyone, she took Hansel and Gretel deep into the forest and abandoned them, leaving them to fend for themselves, so she and the father would have enough food."

Cooper's eyes filled up with tears and he said, "Grandma, their mother left them out there alone, without food? That's terrible."

"No, sweetheart, it was the beginning of intermittent fasting."

"Why didn't Hansel and Gretel run back home?"

"They wanted to. Hansel brought breadcrumbs with him and dropped them all along the way, leaving a trail so they'd know their way back. But Hansel wasn't that smart—if he hadn't wasted the bread, they wouldn't have been abandoned to begin with, and he didn't take into account that the breadcrumbs might get eaten by birds, and he and Gretel would be lost."

"Is that what happened, Grandma?"

"That's exactly right, Kevin."

"My name is Cooper."

"Okay, fine. Details. Anyway, Hansel and Gretel were walking through the forest when they came upon a beautiful house made out of gingerbread, with a roof made of icing and flowers made of candy."

"So Hansel and Gretel ate the candy and gingerbread so they wouldn't be hungry?"

"No, they didn't."

"Why not?"

"They were still in fasting mode. So, they knocked on the door and the old lady who lived there invited them in."

"Was the old lady you?"

My mother was momentarily taken aback by Cooper's innocent, yet deliciously snarky question.

"Melissa, can we give him back to the agency?"

"Mom, he wasn't adopted. You know that."

"Grandma, tell me more of the story."

"Grandma? It's Mrs. Rosenberg to you. Anyway, Cooooper, Hansel and Gretel go into the gingerbread house where the old lady immediately gives them dinner. Not kosher, but not milk with meat, either, so it was fine, even though it was a little heavy on the salt. (Gretel knew she would not be able to get her rings on in the morning.) Little did the children know, but the witch only gave them food so she could fatten them up and eat *them!*"

Cooper's eyes opened wide with shock. "Oh no, is that true, Gran...Mrs. Rosenberg?"

"Would I lie to you?"

Although Cooper was only a young tot, he paused to consider answering her, but decided to move on. (Even at that young age, his internal clock told him "now is not the time to confront Nana." Wise beyond his years.) "Was the witch kosher?"

"Hahaha, you kill me, Canter. No, the witch wasn't even Jewish. Jews don't live in the woods, we live by the beach, you know that. And why do the Jews live near the beach, young man?"

"Because of the sun, Grandma. Not only can we get a nice tan—and everyone looks thinner with a little color—but if we get too much sun, we'll develop sunspots or possibly, God-willing, non-malignant melanoma, and we'll need to see a good dermatologist...and as everyone knows, *all* of the best dermatologists moved from Manhattan or the Five Towns to beach communities after their wives mysteriously died in skiing accidents. Right?"

"And...?"

"And...that means there are lots of rich, single doctors living near the beach?"

I hadn't seen my mother smile like that since Jerry Lewis failed to sell tickets in Vegas and had his entire residency canceled. "Melissa, you have taught him well, Obi-Wan! I am proud!"

She went back to her story. "So, the witch made Gretel a slave and locked Hansel in a cage, where she gave him lots of food to fatten him up.

"Well, the day came when the witch was going to have Hansel for dinner. But since the witch had been on Weight Watchers, she was really hungry and thought, 'Fuck it; I'll eat Gretel too! How many points could she be?' So, the witch asked Gretel to go the front of the oven to see if the fire was hot enough. But Gretel, who was waaaay smarter than her handsome brother—think Ivanka and Don Jr.—figured out what was going on and pretended she didn't understand. Crazed with hunger, the agitated witch decided to show Gretel how to do it. The witch walked over to the open oven and leaned in. And Gretel gave the witch a giant shove, pushing her into the oven and locking the door behind her! That night, for dinner, Hansel and Gretel had a delicious witch au gratin with a side of gingerbread."

"That was a great story, Grandma. Did Hansel and Gretel live happily ever after?"

"It depends on what you consider 'happy.' Did they get their own network series with international distribution rights? No. Did they go on *The Price is Right* and pick the right door and win lots of money or a set of handsome Samsonite Luggage? No.

"In fact, Hansel's story ended up not being happy at all. Turns out, Hansel was a compulsive overeater. Probably stuffing his feelings to cover what must have been very traumatic abandonment issues, Hansel ate so much of the house and the roof that he developed type 2 diabetes. And since they didn't have dialysis in those days, his blood sugar and insulin levels were always going crazy. By the time he was nineteen, due to the diabetes, Hansel went blind and wandered off into the forest, never to be seen again. There were rumors that he'd mistaken a brown bear for a husky Polish woman named Ilka, married her, and had a litter of very Eastern Bloc-looking cubs, but that was just talk. Take it for what you will."

"And what about Gretel?"

"Gretel's life was a little happier, Casper. Due to her herculean strength, she eventually became a star on the German National Men's shot-putting team and wound up winning many medals and fathering five children. She also had LASIK surgery, which was a game-changer.

"Thank you, Grandma. That was a great story. Could you tell me one more? Could you tell me the story of 'Little Red Riding Hood' and the 'Big Bad Wolf'?"

"Of course, Corky. But it wasn't really a big bad wolf. It was the Wolfs, a family who lived down the block from Little Red Riding Hood, a couple of miles outside the city. And while Mr. Wolf was fairly nice—he ran a small, non-chartered airline—Mrs. Wolf was big and bad..."

I told you she loved him.

The Last Supper

As soon as Cooper was potty-trained, my mother started a tradition called, "Grandma Week," where she would take him on a memory-making vacation. On one of the Grandma Weeks, my mother took Cooper to Rome. Their first stop was the Circus Maximus. It nearly became their last stop, when Cooper innocently asked, "Grandma, Mommy said you used to four-wall this place; is it true?"

"Yes, dear, I did."

"In 357 BC, Grandma?" Cooper asked innocently. I later heard that a passing tourist pried her fingers off his neck. Then they were off to their next stop, the Vatican.

My mother tried explaining to Cooper that the Vatican was not only the seat of the Catholic church and home of the pope, it was also known as the Holy See. Cooper said, "Wow, Nana! Does that mean the pope is related to Kathy Griffin, because you call her The F-ing C." Too cute. Isn't genetics wonderful? Nature? Nurture? It's all a mystery.

The Vatican is like Versailles or the Louvre or Kylie Jenner's Instagram account—way too much to see in one day. So, my mother took him to the main hot spots: St. Peter's Square, the Sistine Chapel, and, of course, the gift shop.

Cooper looks like he's in a hostage video. To this day I have no idea what my mom just said to him.

Needless to say, the gift shop was their favorite. Amazing inventory—rosaries, statues, medals, jewelry, and crucifixes of all kinds: wood, metal, silver-plated, St. Benedictine...they even had an autographed crucifix from Madonna's "Papa Don't Preach" tour.

But the item that grabbed Cooper's attention was the Last Supper Talking Clock. I'm not kidding—it really exists; in fact, my mother bought one. Each apostle is given a different time, and when their hour comes, a candle lights up in front of them and they recite a proverb. Talk about a miracle!

When Cooper first saw the clock, he thought it was a photo taken at one of my mom's shows. "Grandma, this looks like your audience; lots of men in dresses!"

I'd like to point out that, even though there was a limited supply of clocks, my mother, nevertheless, began to *hondle* and bargain with the sales nun behind the counter. She tried slipping her a couple of QVC earrings, seeing if the good sister would just damage the frame ever so slightly and give her a discount. "Is it cheaper if Judas stutters? What if we get rid of two of the apostles, and maybe Paul goes twice? How about that slightly damaged clock over there; the ones with Jesus's hands stuck at 6:30? Every time it rings, it looks like he's jerking off."

While in line at the cash register, my mother told Cooper the story of the Last Supper. "For starters, Coop, it was the Last Brunch; if you look closely, you can see that it's daytime. Not only that, but someone with Jesus's personal style would never, *ever* serve mimosas past noon. (Not that it bothered that old lush, Paul, who carried around a hip flask of Thunderbird. FYI, that hip flask is now considered a most holy relic by the Russian Orthodox Church.) It was the day before Christ died and then came back. Which was a miracle."

"Why was it a miracle, Nana? I've seen you die lots of times; you always come back."

"That's on stage, darling—and remember, it's *always* the audience's fault. Anyway, Jesus knew he was going to get crucified the next day, so he had all of his friends come over at noon for a nice, low-fat meal, and to play some games, like Scrabble, Charades, and Which One of You is Going to Screw Me Over and Nail Me to a Cross? As parties go, on a scale of one to ten, I'd give it an eight. The catering was solid, but parking, as always, was an issue. Nevertheless, it was deemed important enough that it's now celebrated in the Vatican, the seat of Catholicism."

After begrudgingly paying full price, my mother patted Cooper on the head, muttered something about the church "not honoring her Writers Guild discount," and walked out.

"And now, my love, it's time to leave the Vatican and head to the seat of Judaism."

"Jerusalem, Grandma?"

"No, sweetheart; Bloomingdale's."

Empty Nest

In the 1980s, there was a sitcom called *Empty Nest*, about a doctor whose adult children move in after his wife dies to help him cope with suddenly being alone. It starred Richard Mulligan and Dinah Manoff and was created by Susan Harris (*Golden Girls*, *Soap*), so you knew it would be funny. And it was. Very funny. However, my son Cooper went away to college this past August, making me an empty-nester, and I can tell you that there's nothing funny about it.

When Cooper began packing his bags (which I had to repack three times), I flashed back to the time when I was preparing to go away to college. I was desperately worried about my mother. According to her, we did everything together; she was not only my mom, she was my BFF. Lucky me.

I remember the day I left like it was yesterday...

I walked into the kitchen, where my mother was gently berating the cleaning lady for "missing a spot," and I said, "Mom, I'm worried about you. Will you be okay when I'm gone?" She smiled and through fake tears said, "No need to worry; I'll be fine, Maureen." Before I could remind her that my name was Melissa, she turned to the cleaning lady and said, "Betty, don't dare push that refrigerator back into place without wiping down the coils in the back." Even though she kept saying, "I'll be fine, I'll be fine," I knew in my heart she was lying to protect me.

A little back story: whenever I was faced with big, life-changing decisions, I'd immediately call my mother and ask for her advice. I don't know why, and neither do multiple therapists. And she always gave it. It was usually wrong and invariably untrue, yet still, for some inexplicable reason, I continued to ask anyway. But since Mom died in 2014, the only way I can speak to her now is if I go to the cemetery and start shoveling. Which, as a Jewish girl, is never going to happen; we don't shovel.

But I found myself in an unpredicted conundrum. After my mother died, I decided to sell my home in Pacific Palisades, which I'd lived in for twenty years, and start fresh.

I bought this big house in Santa Monica for me and Cooper and my long-time BF to live in. And it *is* a big house; on a scale of clown car-to-mansion, it's a seven. It's much too big a house to live in, alone...which is where I find myself today. You see, the BF became an ex-BF and moved out, and as I've mentioned above, my beloved son went off to start his freshman year in college, in some faraway land called "Ohio." Even the foreign exchange student who was living with us moved out and went back to the mysterious country halfway around the world that he came from, also known as Canada. So, other than staff members and gardeners and workers who are there during the day, I'm all alone in the big house. The urge to rip up plants or break shit, just to have company, is overwhelming.

Having a big house is a nice thing but being alone in it has its downsides: For starters, once everyone clocks out, there's no one to yell at. I could yell at my dogs, but that would be totally pointless because they ignore me completely as it is. I can't scream at the neighbors or they'll call the police or, even worse, TMZ.

Having a glass of wine in front of a crackling fire with a loved one is both romantic and soothing; having a glass of wine *alone* in front of a crackling fire is both sad and a stepping-stone to rehab.

My therapist (yes, I have a therapist—any wonder why?) suggested I could ease some of the loneliness by starting a book club, and have the members come to my house once a week. I pointed out that I live in LA—the only things people here read are scripts, prescriptions, and obituaries. A neighbor suggested maybe it would be good for me to host Weight Watchers parties in my den. Hahaha. A bunch of digestion-challenged friends purging on my Restoration Hardware coffee table? I think not. I also think I need new friends.

It finally dawned on me that I could do what my mother did when I went off to gain a higher education. On my first visit home on winter break, when I found out that she had rented out my room—sort of the first Airbnb—I was shocked. I said, "Ma, where am I supposed to sleep?" She said, "Your room, sweetheart; there's no one in it right now." I sighed and gave her a hug. She hugged me back and said, "It'll be ninety-eight dollars a night. Fresh towels and linens provided...

Betty, get the nice sheets and put them in room number four; we have a VIP! Don't look so shocked, Melanie; some homeless vagabond with yellow teeth and matted hair gets a nice place to stay for a few nights and I get his SSI check; it's a win-win!"

For those of you who think my mother had a good idea and that maybe I *should* rent out Cooper's room as a B&B— you're right. It was a good idea, and it turns out my mother wasn't lying when she said she'd be fine in the empty nest. It looks like I'm going to be fine too.

FYI, Cooper's cool with all this and he seems to have turned into a fine little negotiator. He now gets 15 percent of first dollar earned. So proud.

But on those days when I really do miss him, I head down to the local arcade where I can enjoy teenagers rolling their eyes at me in disgust and revulsion. Nothing like feelings of shame and self-loathing to fill the void; it makes me feel right at home.

LIAR

PINOCCHIO

Dear Melissa,

Up until Bill Clinton said, "I did not have sex with that woman" (maybe he was confused and mistook Monica's vagina for a humidor), fictional Italian puppet and child star Pinocchio had always been the gold standard of lying. He was considered the best in his field, the Michael Jordan of fibbing, the Tom Brady of bullshit, the Tiger Woods of whatthefuck? He is so identified with lying that professional fact-checkers rate the egregiousness of lies in "Pinocchios" instead of stars. One Pinocchio is probably a small, little white lie ("Gee, Grandma, this liver compote is really delicious"), whereas a five-star Pinocchio lie is probably fraught with brazenness and consequence ("Of course the baby's yours; yes, I know he's Black and you're Finnish, but wow, those recessive genes, huh?").

For those of you who don't know the story of Pinocchio (perhaps as a child you were kidnapped by a strange hillbilly couple and kept underfed and dirty in a dimly lit basement, or your parents joined a religious cult and only read you books and stories that would help you climb up the bridge to level Clear), here it is, in a nutshell:

Pinocchio was a wooden marionette in Tuscany, Italy, who had a penchant for lying; every time he lied, his nose grew. Eventually, he looked more like a woodpecker than a real boy. No matter how much people told him to tell the truth he just kept lying. Perhaps because he only spoke Italian and we were all speaking English, we just thought he was lying, or perhaps because he couldn't help himself because he had OCD issues. (In addition to lying, perhaps he had to obsessively untangle his strings or varnish his hands six hundred times a day; who knows?)

As a rule, parents teach their children to tell the truth. Like pretty much every other mother in the world, I can't count the number of times I've said to you, "If you tell me the truth, I won't be mad at you; just don't lie to me." Which is of course, total bullshit. You could've absolutely told the truth, but because I said I wouldn't get mad and my word has to be good, I was forced to hold my tongue and say things like, "Sweetheart, I'm sorry you set fire to your school and I appreciate your honesty but I'm disappointed in the decision you made."

Mothers always know when their child is lying...call it a sixth sense, like shopper's intuition. Yes, shopper's intuition is a thing, and yes, I have it. Or should I say I've been blessed with it. Like how people with arthritis know when rain is coming, or the way dogs know if a train is coming down the tracks from a mile away. To this day, I intuitively know if a store anywhere in the continental United States is having a sale, mark-down, coupon rebate, or season-busting-end-of-year giveaway. One time, I was flying from Palm Springs to Palm Beach (or, as I like to think of it, going from entertaining old Jews to entertaining old WASPS). There was a designer jewelry sale going on in the Harry Winston boutique in the Galleria Mall in Houston. I intuitively knew that diamond drop earrings were being marked down and that I had to get to the mall ASAP, before some smooth-talking Southern Belle beat me there and swiped them up. Now, I couldn't tell the pilot we needed to make an emergency landing because I needed to accessorize properly, so I pretended I needed to get to the Houston Heart Clinic ASAP, to see Dr. Michael DeBakey, the nation's foremost heart doctor and a close family friend. Truth be told, I had met him only once, but given my low standards for friendship, technically I was fudging more than fibbing.

Mike and I were at a hospital fundraiser ("V is for Valve!") and we got into an argument over whether or not walnuts are good for cholesterol. Dr. DeBakey believed that walnuts could indeed have a minor, positive impact on heart health, but just because he has a degree from Tulane University doesn't mean he's always right. I've watched every episode of *ER* and *Grey's Anatomy*, and I believe walnuts are bad for your health. Why? Because my friend Jeanette once had walnuts as a snack, and twenty minutes later she was hit by falling masonry and killed as she crossed the street. That's why.

The point is, I bent the truth enough that I was able to make a commercial airliner make an emergency landing so I could go shopping. Top that, Pinocchio!

As for the actual story of Pinocchio, well, sweetheart, I have no idea why they let kids read that crap. The author, Carlo Collodi, completely missed the mark and didn't understand subtle nuanced differences between the protagonist and the antagonist. The focus of the story *should* have been on Geppetto, not Pinocchio, as he was the one who drove the story.

Melissa, Geppetto was a destitute wood carver who made puppets to try and support his wife and family. Already you can see he's a dunce, right?

There were a million things Geppetto could have carved out of wood that had great market value, like floors, lamps, chairs, tables...but no, this idiot wanted to make puppets and marionettes. Be honest, what kind of a market is there for that? How many fucking puppeteers could there be in Italy at one time? Ten? Twenty? How many puppets could he sell, a hundred, maybe? One fifty if you include carnival prizes and men who drive windowless vans?

And do you know how long it takes to carve a puppet? And I mean good ones, not like those pieces of shit Jeff Dunham throws on his knee and makes talk. And by the way, Missy, can you explain how Jeff Dunham has a gazillion-dollar deal for a Vegas residency? I can't. To me that's a bigger mystery than dry ice.

Anyway, it takes weeks to make a puppet, especially if it's a good, hard wood. No wonder Geppetto was destitute. I can't tell you how many times his wife Lillian said, "I beg you, Geppy, please change your medium! Work in clay or vinyl or even hard plastic. We can't go on like this for much longer. I'm running out of Spaghetti Helper!"

You know what would have been a good idea? If Geppetto made it so that every time Pinocchio lied, instead of his nose growing, his penis would grow. Or as they say in Latin, shlongus growus. Women all over Italy would have bought that puppet, not to mention a secondary market of gay men, bi-curious husbands, and scores of local priests. Ka-ching! And, instead of being known as the Pauper Puppetmaster, he would've been known as the Wealthy Wizard of Wood.

Don't "Play Ball!"

For as long as I can remember, I've loved sports. Football, baseball, basketball, hockey, tennis...makes no difference, I love them all and I watch them all. I go from ESPN to ESPN2 to ESPN3 to ESPN47. I'll actually watch a soccer match on ESPN Deportes even though I hate soccer and don't speak a word of Spanish. Just ask my high school Spanish teacher.

When I'm really desperate and in need of a sports fix, I'll actually watch poker on television. How pathetic is that? I'm not playing the game but there I am, in my den, glued to the TV, trying to figure if Buckskin Billy is going to raise on a pair of nines, or fold and let Vinny from Jersey take the pot. Just for the record, I'm curious to know when watching people play cards on TV became a thing. I understand watching people play cards when you're drunk in a casino in Vegas, but when you're home alone on your couch? For starters, poker is not a sport, it's a game. Think of it as golf with chairs instead of carts. (No need to correct me, I know golf *is* a sport; I hear that from my golfer friends all the time. But my question is this: if you can drive from hole to hole, wear plaid pants with white shoes, weigh three hundred pounds and still be competitive, is it really a sport or is it more of a hobby that makes you sweat? Donald Trump plays golf; would you consider him an athlete? Asking for a friend.)

This leads me to wonder if ESPN may actually be the cause of obesity in America. Not fast food, not Big Gulps, not Sara Lee, but ESPN because of their 24/7 coverage of every possible sport under the sun. Instead of playing sports, we're all just sitting and watching. I'm no doctor, nor do I play one on television, but I imagine participating in curling is better for one's health than watching curling.

According to my mother, who many of you didn't know was a curling enthusiast, curling is a great "sport" when compared to luge. Allow me to explain: my parents and I were watching the Winter Olympics one year, I think it was 1980 at Lake Placid. Americans Tai Babilonia and Randy Gardner were favorites to win the gold medal in pairs figure skating. They had to withdraw when Randy pulled a groin muscle. It was his own, so no need for snark. (I remember how the announcer Dick Button used to say, "Tai and Randy, Tai and Randy," with such dripping reverence and feeling you knew that he either really loved them or they had a sex tape of him with an undersized Alpine goat.) Anyway, we finished watching skating, and the two-man luge competition came on. I found it thrilling. Two guys hurtling down an icy course, taking banked curves at a hundred miles per hour, trying not to flip over and possibly kill themselves. I remember getting really excited and yelling, "Mom, check out this luge race; it's the greatest sport ever!"

She stopped what she was doing (updating her phone book by erasing the names of people who had died or people who had slighted her that she now considered dead), looked up briefly, and said, "Melissa, that's not a sport, it's an activity."

"Activity? What are you talking about?"

"Sweetheart, this is nothing new. I've seen this a thousand times before. Two men in skintight spandex outfits, lying on top of each other and screaming. It's either ballet, musical theater, or an after-party at David Geffen's house."

I couldn't believe she didn't get it. Actually, I could. Fortunately, fifteen minutes later, ABC switched coverage from luge to women's downhill skiing. And I say fortunately, because I knew my mother enjoyed watching other women go downhill...mostly pretty actresses, sexy singers, and network executives. To be honest, my parents liked skiing; we had actually gone on skiing vacations. I took ski lessons while they sat and read books in the lodge. (Honestly, my father read books; my mother read the *National Enquirer*. Like I said, it was vacation.) I became pretty good, but my mother always made sure I didn't get *too* good. She thought I only needed to get good enough to...you know, have fun, wear winter white, and hang around the chalet drinking champagne with good-looking, European men wearing expensive sweaters and Rolex watches. She definitely didn't want me to become a full-time skier or any kind of professional athlete.

"Melissa, female athletes have fun and look great, but they rarely get married and, when they do, the marriages rarely last. 'Why, you ask?'"

"I didn't ask why."

"Because being married to a female athlete is too much stress for most husbands, especially if she's the breadwinner. She's traveling the world, making millions of dollars playing golf, and he's home playing househusband, scouring sinks, washing floors, and fighting waxy, yellow buildup. If you think he had a small shlong before she cashed her paycheck..."

"Melissa, men are intimidated by athletic women, especially when the man isn't athletic. Take your father, for example; he wasn't athletic; I mean, he was British, for God's sake. All he could do was outrun raindrops. If Dad and I ever got into a boxing match or arm-wrestling tournament, I'd have kicked his ass. But I loved him too much to do that; I didn't want to intimidate him with my natural, God-given physical tools, so I just pretended I wasn't athletic to make him feel better."

"Mom, you *pretended* to be unathletic? Exactly how stupid do you think I am?"

"Well..."

"Mom, not for nothing, but you are not athletic. In fact, you're kind of a spaz. No one ever said, 'That Joan; what a gazelle.'"

My mother gasped, put her hand to her mouth, and looked horrified as though she'd just witnessed an assassination or found out that a younger female comic got a gig she wanted. She turned white, and I think I saw her eyes roll a little bit back in her head. I thought surely I'd crossed the line and hurt her feelings by calling her a spaz. But I was wrong.

"Melissa! What did I tell you about using double negatives! Who speaks like that, a peasant? All that money on private schools and you speak English like a deaf Russian. I am livid!"

Strangely, I felt better.

The only sport other than skiing that my parents allowed was horseback riding. I guess they noticed that I'd always loved horses. I don't know why I loved horses—maybe it was because they're so big and powerful yet also so silky and gentle; they're kind of like Lizzo with better hair.

It all started when I was five years old. Secretariat won the Triple Crown of horse racing: the Kentucky Derby, the Preakness, and the Belmont Stakes. Even though I was young, watching him win the Belmont by thirty-one lengths gave me goosebumps. When he crossed the finish line, my entire family jumped up and cheered and exchanged high-fives. I was so excited. I said, "Mommy, that's what I want to do!"

"Be mounted and ridden by a small man with a whip?" she replied.

"No, I want to ride horses."

"Oh, okay. You know what? You can ride horses but not race them. Racing is too dangerous. How about jumping?"

"Okay." So, I got up off the couch and started jumping.

"Not you, the horses."

So, my parents bought me a horse and gave me riding lessons. I entered competitions and, over the years, I actually won some ribbons.

My first horse was named Toby. He was really sweet. A perfect first horse. At least I thought so; my mother, not so much.

"Melissa, Toby is a lovely horse, very nice. But he's not perfect. You know who's a perfect horse? Mr. Ed, that's who.

"Now, Mr. Ed may not jump, but he talks. And I don't mean horse-talk, you know, whinny, whinny, neigh, neigh, I mean real talking."

"I know. I've seen him on TV. But isn't that fake?"

Continuing on as though I hadn't asked a question, my mother said, "Admittedly, he has kind of an annoying, flat Midwest accent, but still it's pretty amazing. And you know what's really amazing? He appreciates good etiquette. He likes to be called *Mister* Ed; not the less formal 'Ed,' or, God forbid, 'Eddie,' but Mister Ed; how's that for class, huh? Plus...and this is the super-duper amazing thing about him... he's worth a fortune! Mister Ed stars in a prime-time television show, he gets residuals for syndication, he takes an additional producer/writer credit, and he has a back-end participation deal that includes international distribution!

"Don't get me wrong, sweetheart, I adore Toby. He jumps, he canters, he brushes flies off his ass with his tail, all the regular horse stuff. Not to mention that he can shit when he walks; you know how much I love multitasking. Toby is a wonderful horse, but if you could somehow teach him to talk, he'd be perfect. Even if he has an unusually high-pitched voice, it would still be great. And if you can also teach him sign language, jackpot! I could sell that to a network as diversity programming."

I just smiled and nodded, hoping those non-verbal cues would prevent my mother from changing her mind or continuing to talk. I was 50 percent successful. She kept talking.

"Melissa, do you know why I said yes to horseback riding? Because you're not the athlete, the horse is. You're just the gorgeous arm candy—or should I say, fetlock candy? Men will be impressed, not intimidated. And the men you'll meet will be horsemen. I don't mean well-hung, I mean well-financed.

"Now do you understand what I'm talking about, Missy? Athlete adjacent: good. Actual athlete: bad.

"Do you realize that Dorothy Hamill has been married and divorced twice, gone bankrupt, and been thrown out of the Ice Capades? She doesn't even have money for a hairstylist anymore. I mean, my God, Little Dot's had the same wedge cut for forty-seven fucking years. She needs to come up with a few bucks for a trip to Supercuts. Anything would be better than that schoolgirl things she's been working since 1976. I have an idea, Missy; Dorothy should throw herself down on the ice, fake a knee injury and meet a nice orthopedist, and live happily ever after.

I was horrified.

"Don't look at me like that; not so far-fetched. That's what Sandy Duncan did. Sandy needed a glass eye, so she married an ophthalmologist. Brilliant! Surgery, glass eye, and Windex; didn't cost her a fucking dime.

"And what about Billie Jean King and her husband, Larry King? Needless to say, that marriage fell apart. Although that may not have been her fault; Larry was really old and decrepit."

"Mom, that's a different Larry King. She wasn't married to the call-in talk show host—and Billie Jean and Larry didn't get divorced because she's athletic, they got divorced because she's gay."

"Hello, Vagina, you're on the air."

"Mom, you're being ridiculous; female athletes can have wonderful marriages and lead happy, healthy lives."

"But not long ones. Remember Ruffian?"

"The racehorse?"

"Of course, the racehorse, Melissa. How many other women named Ruffian do you know? Poor Ruffian, poor single, unattached Ruffian...died of a broken heart, at only three years old."

"Mom, that is not true. Ruffian had to be euthanized after she broke down during a race. It was horrible."

"Oh sure, that's the story they tell you. But the truth is, Ruffian took her own life. Poor thing was very depressed because she couldn't find a stud. None of the male horses—not a one, not even the lazy, old, three-legged palomino named 'Glue Factory' would toss her a hump. None of them wanted to go out with her because she was too butch. Like all men, they were intimidated by a female athlete.

"One dewy summer morning, the trainers went into Ruffian's stall to walk and feed her and found the poor girl hooves up with a note on the bale of hay beside her that read, 'Tell

Melissa Rivers not to go into sports. She'll intimidate men and wind up alone.' Now *that's* horrible!"

I was stunned. My mother's "storytelling" had reached dizzying new heights. I didn't know what to say. So I said nothing. I went to my room and turned on the TV to ESPN94. They were airing the early rounds of an Italian bocce ball tournament. I watched the entire thing, even though I don't like bocce ball and I don't speak Italian; just ask my high school Italian teacher.

For the record and much to my mother's chagrin, I was a multi-sport athlete in high school and remain athletic to this day.

I am also still single.

Maybe she was right. Dear God, help me.

Again, with the Sports?

M twenty-one-year-old son, Cooper (YES, he's twenty-one!), goes to college to play lacrosse. Before I go on, I realize that that sentence is fraught with tension and must've put a couple of questions in your mind. Allow me to answer:

1. Yes, Cooper is twenty-one, and yes, I know that seems impossible given that I'm only thirty-one. (Play along with me here; I'm sensitive, okay?) Time flies. It seems like only yesterday that he was a cute kid, scowling at me from the other room when I asked him if he did his homework. Now he's a cute adult who scowls at me from the computer screen when I ask him if he's done anything at all. He's two years away from graduation, which means he has two years left to call me "Mom," after which he has to introduce me to people as either his older sister or his lesbian Aunt Pat, who just moved to California from Vermont. (Yes, he'll be lying; what's your point?)

2. Yes, he's going to college to play lacrosse. There are a lot of reasons people attend college, and sometimes academics is one of them. But not always. Cooper hasn't

declared a major yet (he's only a sophomore), but he's been advised that sleeping, eating, and drinking are not actually listed as fields of study. He'll eventually find a major that he likes and build a career off of that. (Let's just hope he doesn't pick medicine; how would you feel if the man holding the scalpel over your head became a brain surgeon begrudgingly because he had trouble scoring goals on a power play?)

3. Lacrosse, surprisingly, is hugely popular in North America, especially in Canada, where it is the national sport. Did you know that? I'll bet you didn't; I'll bet you thought it was hockey, like I did. But nay, nay, *mes amis*, lacrosse is Canada's national pastime. This confusion is all across the continent. Most Americans think that baseball is our national pastime, but it isn't, gossiping is. (And yes, gossiping *is* a sport; if done properly, you can absolutely raise your heart rate.) Think I'm kidding? More people gossip than play shortstop for the Dodgers. I rest my case. *Everyone*—with the possible exception of clergy—wait, no, they gossip too. (What do you think they talk about after finishing Communion? God? No, they talk about the ugly hat in the third pew.) Children talk behind one another's backs, while teens' very lifeblood is betraying friends' secrets they'd sworn to keep. Even old people gossip, although in many cases they're too aged to actual dis someone, so when a person's name is mentioned, they just shake their heads and mutter things like, "That sonuvabitch," or, "She never should have married him; I never liked him."

My mother never liked sports at all, let alone lacrosse. She had no idea what it was. Every weekend for ten years, Cooper would leave the house in his uniform, going to either a game or a practice. As he headed out the door, he'd yell, "Bye, Grandma," and my mother would look up from her bank statement and say, "So long, Carl; have fun!"

Once he was out of hearing distance, she'd say, "Melissa; why does he always wear the same outfit? It's not right. People are going to think you're in the poor house or don't want to do laundry, and that reflects badly on me. When I come off stage, audience members will mutter, 'Oh sure, she's funny, but she lets her grandson dress like a hobo. What kind of a person does that?' I once heard a woman say, 'All those lovely clothes Joan sells on QVC, yet she lets that boy walk around like a vagabond in those dingy shorts? Appalling.' Melissa, your son Claude looking like a ragamuffin is going to kill my online sales. For fuck's sake, in the name of God, do something! Make him wear a different outfit once in a while!"

I can hear your shock through the pages as you're reading. I tried explaining it all to my mother one Saturday afternoon, after Cooper had left for a game. We were sitting in the den, watching an old videotape of Princess Diana's funeral (it always made my mother feel good; she loved parades), judging which royals were mourning honestly and which ones were just putting it on for the cameras, when I said, "Mom, do you know where Cooper just went?"

"No," she said, "but I know he was in that same filthy outfit again."

"Mom, it's not an outfit. It's a uniform."

"Uniform? Like prisoners wear? Do you remember the movie *Schindler's List*? Of course you do; we showed it at your sweet sixteen party as part of our 'Never Forget' theme. Anyway, in the movie, all of the people in the camps wore striped pajamas and all of the Nazis wore black leather. It was like a very strict fetish night at the Ramrod. The only pop of color in the whole fucking movie was that little girl in the red dress; soooooo obvious."

"Cooper's wearing a sports uniform, not a prison or military uniform. Not only criminals wear uniforms, Mom. Cooper plays on a lacrosse team."

I could see by the look on her face that she had no idea what lacrosse was. Nor did she care.

"Missy, you know who always wore the same outfit...I mean *uniform*? Superman. Every goddamned day, he would start out in the same bland, off-the-rack, non-designer suit complete with hat and tie, and then go into a phone booth and come out in a red and blue nylon onesie with a cape. He does it once? Interesting. Twice? Something's going on here. Three times? He's clearly got no money, and is definitely not marriage material..."

"...Ma..."

"I do think the cape was a nice idea, especially for evenings, but *all* the time? No! Loses its senses of importance and whimsy."

"Mom! Lacrosse is a sport, like baseball. You've gone to baseball games at Yankee Stadium, right? Didn't you notice that all of the players were wearing the same thing?"

"Well, of course, I did, Missy, but all of the uniforms had numbers on them, like limited editions of a painting, which makes each one different and unique. And Melissa, surprise, surprise—I know how the whole uniform numbering thing in baseball began!"

"Everyone knows that, Mom. The players' uniform numbers corresponded with their place in the batting order."

"Well then, Melissa, everyone doesn't know shit. The numbers corresponded alright, but *not* with the batting order."

Before I could jump in with a question, she continued, "I knew both Babe Ruth and Mickey Mantle *very*, *very* well, if you know what I mean."

"You slept with Babe Ruth and Mickey Mantle? Seriously?"

"Let me tell you, there's a reason why Ruth wore three and the Mick wore seven. My only regret in life is not having had a turn with Reggie Jackson; he wore forty-four. Can you imagine? My God, Mr. October..."

As I got up to go to the bathroom and vomit, one thought crossed my mind: Thank God my mother doesn't understand lacrosse or have any interest in it. If she did, Cooper's coach might be a marked man.

Anne Frank

When I was twelve or thirteen, we took a family vacation and went all over the world. One of our favorite places was Europe. My father (who was raised in London) was so excited for me to see all of the important European sites: Buckingham Palace, Westminster Abbey, The Eiffel Tower, the Roman Colosseum, the Paris Opera House, the canals of Venice, all of it. The part my mother was most excited for me to see were the Nazi concentration camps—not because she thought it was important to understand our family heritage, but because she wanted to be able to play a fun new car game on family road trips that she called, "What's the Most Underrated Concentration Camp?" ("Melissa, I think Mauthausen never got its just due, and Drancy, the French transfer camp, was oh so much more than just an ugly building complex in a shitty neighborhood.")

My father was a ridiculously smart man and, at every landmark, he'd tell me facts about the place to put it in its historical context. Yes, my mother was really smart too, but facts bored her. By the end of a full day of sightseeing, she would be on fire and just start making shit up. For example:

My mother "socializing"—he's clearly not rich, single, or able to help her career.

Dad: "Melissa, did you know that the Eiffel Tower was named for Gustave Eiffel, an architect and engineer, whose firm designed the tower for the 1889 World's Fair?"

Mom: "Melissa, did you know that Gustave Eiffel liked to wear women's panties and be called 'Sally' at weekly Left Bank artists' salons?"

Me: "Dad, is that true?"

Dad: "Which part, Melissa, about the naming or the shaming?"

Mom: "It's not shaming, Edgar...I'm informing. Melissa, it's common knowledge that Gus could design both buildings and outfits. An A-frame or an A-line, made no difference; the man was gifted. (Pause for my dad to roll his eyes.) I'm sure it's all true. If you don't believe me, go ask Eiffel. He'll be at Forgotten Woman, tomorrow at 11:00."

Here's another tale from "Vacationing with the Rosenbergs:" When we visited the Leaning Tower of Pisa, the famed bell tower in Italy, my mother said, "You know, Melissa, they say the tower leans because it was built on an unstable foundation; nonsense! Here's the truth: For starters, it took almost two hundred years to build, which means either the workers were really slow, or they got paid by the hour. And if you really want to see an 'unstable foundation,' spend a couple of hours alone, in a room, with Gary Busey.

"Believe it or not, indirectly it's Elizabeth Taylor's fault that the tower leans. That's right, my best friend, Large Liz. You see, Elizabeth Taylor is a quarter Italian...I did some research and found out that Liz had an ancestor who was a *really* fat woman in Pisa, also named Elizabeth. In fact, the ancestor was so fat, her full name was Elizabeth New Jersey. Anyway, in the year 1398, Elizabeth New Jersey enrolled in a Bikram yoga class that was being held in the top of Pisa's bell tower. One day during class, Elizabeth cramped and got stuck in a yoga pose, Downward Facing Elephant. She couldn't get out if it and because she was so big, no one else could move her either. She was stuck! After three days, the tower began leaning to the left under the strain of Elizabeth's weight, tilting more and more, little by little, inch by inch, as every passing hour went by. By day four,

Royal-ish Wedding

was one of only four Americans at the royal-
ing—and I say royal-*ish* because she was at
Prince Charles and Camilla Parker Bowles,
g of Charles and Diana (which was the royal
other wasn't at Charles's wedding to Lady Di
mother explained to me, "Diana was jealous
she couldn't compete. She'd look at me with
say, 'Lady, die!'" I'm fairly sure that wasn't
ooth my mother and Diana are dead, I can
nor deny.

sk, "Who were the three other Americans?"
em were famous celebrities, which means

oiggest dilemma was what kind of a wedding
o you shop for the future King of England?
t can you buy someone who owns Scotland?
a castle on an estate. With servants. And
for Little Nigel, who's no longer a footman.
wn a dumbwaiter and lost both of his legs,
f being a footman, he's a stumpman. And

however, Elizabeth had sweated off enough Bikram pounds that she could be pushed over, dragged out of the room, and eventually lowered down the side of the tower to safety, like a giant I-beam. And not a moment too soon. Another few hours, and the whole tower would have collapsed and killed God knows how many innocent people. So, now Melissa, you know why Richard Simmons is a millionaire genius. When I tell you to eat salads and count your carbs, now you know why."

Imagine that, a lie and a life lesson, all at the same time. Thanks, Mom.

Anyway, back to the Nazis. Although we didn't get to tour any of the concentration camps on *that* trip (never say never), we did make a stop at Anne Frank's house in Amsterdam. It's important to understand that my mother was obsessed with Anne Frank—in later years, my mom would talk about Anne in her act and write about her in books. I was never sure why, but in hindsight, it might have been a psychological transference. You see, Anne had a sister, Margot, that no one really heard about, but was probably the family favorite. And my mother had a sister named Barbara, who was clearly the family favorite. ("Barbara was the smart one, Barbara was the pretty one, blah blah blah…") I'm not a shrink, nor do I play one on television, but just sayin'…

Having read *The Diary of Anne Frank* (and watched the movie), I expected our visit to the hiding space would be extremely emotional and have a long-lasting impact on me. But I was wrong. You see, my mother decided to give me the "inside dirt" on Anne's story.

It's believed that someone who knew of the Franks's hiding place tipped off the Nazis. This led to their capture and subsequent transport to various camps. But my mother didn't believe it.

"Melissa, what people don't know is that part of the reason the Franks got found out and caught was due to Anne's devotion to dance. Yes, dance! The music was in her soul; it is part of who she was. Fly like a bird she must. Writing was just a side hustle; dance was her life. Throwing caution to the wind, all day, all night, tap, tap, tap, tap, tap...jeté, plié, frappé, whatever. Anne's dancing created a fucking ruckus. I'm surprised that the Franks weren't turned in earlier by the people downstairs.

"All day long, while everybody else in the attic was whispering and shushing and padding around in socks, Anne was tapping her way across the kitchen, down the hall and back. Safety, circumstance, nothing, not even threat of death could stop her from doing a sassy little jitterbug across the attic floor. And there was no dance Anne couldn't do (like Mozart, she was a prodigy). She could tap, she could fandango, she could even do a gentle bossa nova. Anne Frank was Ginger Rogers before there was Ginger Rogers. But I understand; like any true artist, when the muse would speak, there was nothing Anne could do. Talk about dying for your craft.

"In fact, I've heard that Anne's last words as she was being shoveled into the boxcar by the Nazis was a lyric Gene Kelly sang in *Singin' in the Rain*: 'Gotta Dance!'"

I'm pretty sure th
but just to be on th
neighbors again, I w
PS: Due to the cr
attempts at interpr
of head wounds an
which she was forc
concussion protoco

The

My mothe
ish wed
the wedding
not the wedd
wedding). My
because, as m
of me; she kne
daggers as if
true, but sinc
neither confir

Before you
don't; none of
who gives a sh

My mother
gift to get. Ho

"Melissa, w
The man lives
footmen—exce
Poor thing fell
so now, instea

*In Europe. My mother and her friends taking a leisurely walk. I'm
planning my escape route. My mother took her dog, Spike, everywhere
she went. Sometimes she took me too. Why am I so down? Because
my mother's +1 was her dog, Spike.*

since he can no longer fetch things for the prince—at least
not quickly—he now works as a hat rack in the gift shop of
Windsor Castle."

I was on board with this conversation until my mother
started in with the amputee footman story. But I said nothing
and let her continue.

"I wonder where they're registered? Primark? Tedesco?
Bed, Bath & Balmoral?"

"I doubt they're registered anywhere, Mom. My suggestion: forget extravagant, go for something practical. Something
they could use."

"Like what, eight thousand garden gnomes or a moat jockey? Maybe two hundred toaster cozies, you know, one for every kitchen?"

"How about something that would be personal, something special for each of them."

My mother paused, seeming to actually have listened to me and said, "I know! A box of Depends and a pair of earmuffs. Although with his ears, that could cost me a fucking fortune."

"Honestly, Mom, didn't the formal invitation say 'no gifts'?"

"Yes, of course, but no one who puts that on an invitation really means it."

"I do."

"Then you're an idiot. You've missed out on a lot of great gifts...not to mention lots of shitty gifts you can then re-gift when you're invited somewhere and the invitation says, 'no gifts.'"

"Then why not just re-gift them one of the shitty gifts you've gotten?"

"Because I sold them all on eBay, that's why. Slap an autograph on something and it triples its market value. How do you think you got to college?"

"Because I'm smart?"

"Okay, fine, if that makes you happy. Anyway, we'll discuss this again later as we get closer to the date. In the meantime, start looking through *The PennySaver*; see if anything catches your eye."

If you're wondering why my mother was invited to Prince Charles's wedding—and why wouldn't you be, I nearly didn't invite her to mine—it's because she knew him for a million years. There are various versions of how they met, but my mother's version goes like this:

My mom always had a huge following in the UK, and one year she was invited to do a benefit for one of the prince's charities. Of course, she said yes; not because she knew much about the charity, but because she wanted to be in the good graces of the royal family so that, in the event Charles unexpectedly died, she'd be in the will. Unbeknownst to my mother, Charles was actually at the benefit and afterwards came backstage to thank her for her performance.

"So, I'm in the dressing room, taking off my makeup and washing my falsies in the sink when in walks Prince Charles. He's taller than I thought and stoops over a bit—probably from the relentless browbeating he gets from the sourpuss father. He says, 'Joan, may I call you, Joan?'

"I say, 'Sure; it's much better than "lifeless bloodsucker," which is what my husband calls me.'"

"'Thank you so much for doing tonight's child abuse benefit.'

"'Are we for it or against it?'

"He laughed out loud; I guess he thought I was kidding. He tells me we raised over a million pounds for the charity. I wanted to say, 'Why hold a benefit? You're a gazillionaire; why not just sell Wales and donate the proceeds?' But what I said was, 'Oh, that's so great. What kindness and compassion you have for your loyal subjects.' I was going to continue fawning and sucking up but was interrupted by some bandaged and bruised little boy, a street urchin no doubt—who wandered in looking for a bathroom."

"'Scuse me, Mum; is there a men's room nearby?'

"'Get the fuck out of here, Oliver! Does this look like a men's room?'"

Again, Charles must've thought my mother was kidding. He laughed and pointed the boy in the right direction. And then he fell in love with my mother, in spite of all the jokes she told about the royal family.

"Charles has a great sense of humor, Missy. He not only gets the jokes, he's funny. Someday, he'll be the funniest king since Alan.

"Chuck must've gotten his sense of humor from his grandmother, the Queen Mum, because Queen Elizabeth is humorless and Prince Philip was too angry to even be marginally amusing."

"What was Prince Philip so angry about? He had a pretty good life, no?"

"Absolutely. But he was a sourpuss. I get it. It's not easy being married to a rich, famous, successful woman, no matter how secure and evolved a man is. Holding your wife's purse when she's in the mall shopping for shoes can be very emasculating; imagine doing it when your wife is the most famous woman in the world."

"I don't think Queen Elizabeth shops in a mall."

"Really? Have you seen her shoes? Can you imagine being Prince Philip, sitting on a bench in front of Payless, and after two hours, the queen comes out with only two pairs of beige, chunk heels and complimentary support hose? Then demands to go to the food court for a Wetzel's Pretzel? I don't blame him for being crabby. Very typical male behavior."

"Mom, not all men are like that."

"True. Some men handle it very well, like Gerald Ford."

"Mom...he was a president, not just 'some man.'"

"He was president for two years, Melissa; *two*. After that, you never heard from him. Pardons Nixon and vanishes from sight. Jimmy Hoffa was seen more often. But Betty Ford? Huge. Giant TV-Q. People loved her. She drank, she smoked, she had things removed...you could talk to her. She started the most famous rehab in the world. If it wasn't for Betty Ford, Liza Minnelli would still be snorting blow off a bouncer's ass in an alley behind a gay bar in a bad neighborhood.

"Anyway, Camilla Parker Bowles has a great sense of humor too. She's a regular broad. You can curse in front of her. If you say 'cunt' in front of her, she laughs. If you said 'cunt' in front of Diana, she'd blush, and if you say 'cunt' in front of the Queen, she says,

"'Yes, can I help you?'"

"You said 'cunt' in front of The Queen of England? And you wonder why you haven't been invited back to Buckingham Palace."

"It wasn't my fault. I was at a party playing 'what's your safe word' with Margaret Thatcher when the Queen walked by on her way to the toilet. I had no idea she was there."

"Did you apologize?"

"What was I supposed to do, follow her into the ladies' room? You know you're not allowed to speak to the Queen when she's on the throne.

"Cunt aside, Charles and Camilla are actually a perfect match—they both have great senses of humor, they both love each other, and they both have a ton of emotional baggage: he has 'mommy issues,' and she's an old whore."

"For God's sake, Mom, you can't say that about her; she's a duchess!"

"Duchess, schmuchess. They had to give Camilla a title, she was marrying royalty. They couldn't make her a princess, because Diana was a princess, and it would look bad. And she'll never be queen because Elizabeth is never going to die. Never. She's already been queen for like a hundred years. I'm telling you, the woman is like one of those giant sea turtles from the Galapagos; give her a hard shell and some kelp, and she'll live to be a thousand. Secondly, Camilla was married before; how would she be introduced at royal functions? 'Please Welcome Charles, The Prince of Wales, and Camilla, Lady of the Evening, Gay Divorcee?' So, they made her a duchess—which is not such a big deal; there are plenty of duchesses."

"So 'duchess' is like the 'schizophrenia' of royal titles? An umbrella they use for anyone whose lineage and past vocation are questionable?"

But I digress. Back to the actual wedding. The wedding ceremony was separate from the blessing, which was televised, and the private reception that followed. The ceremony was held inside Windsor Castle with just immediate family

and a couple of officials. The queen didn't attend the ceremony; according to my mother, she was "out back having a
wine cooler and a coupla smokes." The blessing and reception were held outdoors on the castle grounds, much to my
mother's dismay; "Nothing to steal; you can't stuff a rock or
tree into your purse."

My mother had a great time at the wedding, in part, I
think, because it was low-key, since both parties had been
married before. (Needless to say, Camilla didn't wear white.
"Melissa, given Camilla's history, she could've worn a leather
mask and had to unzip her mouth in order to say 'I do.'")

Second—or even third—marriages are not unusual for
the royal family. In fact, many royals have had multiple marriages. The most famous is probably Henry VIII, who was
married six times. Seven if you count Anne Boleyn twice,
because he had to bury her twice: her body in a coffin,
her head in a hatbox. Fun fact: After Hank executed Anne
Boleyn, he married Jane Seymour, who went on to have a
long career, highlighted by her lead role in the moderate
TV hit, *Dr. Quinn, Medicine Woman*, which, by the way, she
owned and is still living off of the residuals. The syndication
rights alone made her richer than two-thirds of the royal
family. Have you seen her place in Malibu? Seriously.

And let's not forget Edward VIII, who abdicated the
throne to run off and marry his mistress, Wallis Simpson.
This was shocking even by royal marriage standards. Even
my mother was stunned by this bit of infidelity. "Missy, this
is truly the most amazing thing. I can understand a man
running off with another woman, but *this* woman? Have

you ever *seen* a picture of Wallis Simpson? Grrruff, ruff! A dog! And those were the retouched photos! The wedding was catered by Alpo. After they exchanged 'I dos,' the priest said, 'You may now spay the bride.'

"All I can say is, in order to hook Edward, Wallis must've been able to do some crazy tricks in bed. You know, like pull a rabbit out of her vagina, or turn her yeast infection into sourdough."

"Well, whatever, it worked."

At this point, I saw a glint in her eye that made me realize she was about to go into lecture mode. Desperately, I tried to completely change the subject before she spontaneously combusted.

"Mom, did you finish the *Times* Sunday crossword you were working on...in ink?" Flattery was a shiny object she would absolutely always follow. Except for this time.

"You know Charles and Camilla sent me a postcard from their honeymoon? Do you know where they went? Not some fancy resort on an island, not some mountaintop retreat in the Alps, but a week in the country. His country. The one he owns. Scotland. I guess he didn't have enough frequent flyer points to go to the Bahamas."

"Scotland" brought me right back to the beginning of our conversation. "So, Mom, what *did* you get them as a wedding gift?"

"Nothing, sweetheart, I got them nothing. I decided I'd wait until one of them dies and then buy the survivor a fabulous condolence gift. No one else does that. Think of the publicity I'll get: 'Joan Rivers Makes Royal Farewell a Memorable One.'"

"Okaaay...but what if they die *together* in some freak accident or a murder/suicide pact?"

"Oh my God, I never even thought of that. Melissa, you're a genius! I know! I'll get them his-and-hers parting gifts, just like they do on *The Price is Right*!"

"So, a double funeral is a win-win?"

"Absolutely. Where would I be without you, Missy? You're just like me, you're a chip off the old block!"

"Oy."

JOAN'S FAVORITE "ROYAL" JOKES

1. The royal wedding will be jam-packed with European nobility. The guest list has more blue blood on it than a Smurf slasher film.

2. Kate Middleton is so thin, she had to have her tiara taken in.

3. I feel so sorry for Princess Diana. It's so difficult being a princess when you're not a Jewish American.

4. Fergie is so practical. She's the first woman I ever saw wear a wedding dress with pockets.

5. The closest I ever came to royalty was having my teeth crowned.

6. The queen is a lousy dresser. They rolled out the red carpet and she tried it on.

7. I sympathize with Princess Diana. How would you like to have a mother-in-law with her own army?

8. What surprised me most about Queen Elizabeth and her husband having separate bedrooms was that his was in Scotland.

9. When English people make love and climax, they say, "I have arrived," or ask, "Did you arrive yet?"

10. For the wedding, they needed something old and something blue. They asked me to hold my breath.

"Melissa? Did you bring my big pocketbook? These estate houses have so much stuff to 'borrow.'"

Shalom!

Due to my mother's comedy touring schedule, our family spent a lot of time traveling. Yet, oddly, when she had a break and she was off the road, we'd hit the road.

We loved to go on vacation. And by "we," I mean my mother; my father went along with whatever plans my mother made because it was easier than arguing ("Joan, I'm having chest pains; I can't go to Aruba." "Of course you can, Edgar; we'll take an ambulance to the airport."), and I went along because, well, I was a child, and had little bargaining power. The good news was, we always went somewhere really cool and interesting. Sometimes it was a very fancy-schmancy, five-star resort, and other times it was earthy and rustic. (By the way, I've learned that the concept of "rustic" is far more appealing than actual rustic.)

One year, when I was about eleven, we went to Israel. Now, Israel is not high on the "places I want to go before I die" list of most eleven-year-olds. Admittedly, most eleven-year-olds don't have a "places I want to go before I die" list, but I did—yes, I know that's odd, but work with me here—and

Israel wasn't on it. Monte Carlo, Dubai, and Harrods were. I may have been morbid, but I wasn't stupid.

One night, I think it was the seventeenth night of Chanu-kah (my mother would stretch the holiday season for weeks if she thought she still had a chance of receiving a gift), *ma mère* marched into the den, turned off the TV, and made an announcement.

"Edgar, I have an announcement to make!"

"Then make it. You don't have to announce that you're going to announce something, you just announce it," my father replied.

"Well, then, in that case, I have *two* announcements to make. The first one is, Edgar, because of your lousy attitude, you're not getting laid tonight."

"Who knew I'd be rewarded for a lousy attitude?"

"The second one is, I've decided that on our next family vacation, we're going to Israel!"

I very quickly scanned my mental bucket list of places I wanted to go. I got as far as Sing Sing Prison and the Grassy Knoll (like I said, morbid) when I started getting a headache. So, like a fool, I just blurted out, "Okay, Mom. Why Israel?"

"Thank you for asking, sweetheart. I love you more than anyone else in the room. I want to go to Israel to get back to my roots."

To which my father said, "Well then, sweetheart, shouldn't we go to the Clairol factory?"

And you thought my mother was the funny one.

"Edgar, as Jews, it's important that we embrace our heri-tage and revisit our homeland."

"Mom? You were born in Brooklyn, Daddy was born in Germany, and I was born in California. I'm no Magellan, but I'm pretty sure none of those places are anywhere near Israel."

"Melissa, Melissa, Melissa. These are the times when I look back and think we should have adopted that little Filipino boy instead of you. At least we could have put him to work in the fields. And unlike you, he wouldn't complain about it."

"Mom! I wasn't adopted."

"You don't know that. Anyway, back to more important things. Israel.

"Israel is the home of the Wailing Wall and the Dead Sea. It's where Jesus delivered the Sermon on the Mount. You probably don't know this, but the Sermon on the Mount was the *second*-best speech ever made. The best speech was made by Jesus's cousin, Lenny: The Spiel on the Mountain, which was made in the Catskills, in Kiamesha Lake, three days before Purim. People are still talking."

So, off we went to Israel. If you think the Six-Day War was a traumatic experience...

So, let's start with the Six-Day War. A little backstory: According to the history books, in 1967, Egypt closed the shipping lanes in the Straits of Tiran to Israel. Doing this would damage Israel's trade routes and economy, so Israel retaliated militarily and attacked Egypt and its allies, Jordan and Syria. Six days later (hence the name), Israel won the war and took over the Sinai and the West Bank.

However, according to my mother, the war was actually fought over catering.

"Melissa, territory shmerritory! Jews love food. We love food the way Italians love stuffing people into the trunk of a car."

"Mom, that's a terrible thing to say about Italians. I watch TV. Only the Mafia does that."

"And Frank Sinatra. What do you think was being shipped on the Straits of Tiran? Weapons? Oil? Or food.... Hmmmmm? With the Straits closed, the Israelis would lose access to a million pounds of whitefish, not to mention a ton of kugel and God knows how much brisket. Do you blame them for going to war?"

"Is that true?"

"Of course, it's true. General Moshe Dayan told me himself."

"You knew Moshe Dayan?"

"We had a thing; don't tell your father. Big Mo thought I was gorgeous. Of course, he only had the one eye, so I always made sure he was on my good side. From the left, I'm stunning."

"You had an affair with Moshe Dayan?"

"It wasn't an affair; it was a thing. A three-way, actually, with Golda Meir."

"Why are you telling me this? I'm a child."

"You need to learn the ways of the world sooner than later, Melissa. When they say, 'politics makes strange bedfellows,' they're not kidding."

I must have had that "I think I'm going to throw up" look on my face, because my mother actually backtracked a little.

"Oh Missy, Golda didn't really do much in the three-way. She basically sat naked on a folding chair and had a coupla Luckys, while me and Moshe played, 'Duck, Duck, I'm Going to Goose You.' You know, Golda Meir had the most massive breasts I've ever seen, if you don't count the women in the waiting room in Dr. Cohen's office."

"Who's Dr. Cohen?"

My mother paused as though she'd just witnessed an assassination (of someone she liked) and said, "Who's Dr. Cohen? *Who's Dr. Cohen?*... You know who knows who Dr. Cohen is? That Filipino boy we should have adopted, that's who knows! Do you ever listen, Melissa? Dr. Cohen is the finest breast man in the country. He's done more with breasts than Colonel Sanders. You've never seen his commercials? He's sitting on top of a giant brassiere and he says, 'Hi, I'm Dr. Ben Cohen, The Boob King of Beverly Hills. Every boob is different, but here, one price fits all! At The Boob King, we go tit-for-tat!'"

"How does this have anything to do with Golda Meir?"

"Because I recommended him to her. After one of our afternoon trysts, as Golda was wrestling on her support hose, I leaned over and said, "G, those melons are out of season. I've got a guy who can trim them down and perk them up. You'll never have to walk all hunched over like Quasimodo again."

"What did she say?"

"I have no idea; I couldn't understand a thing she said."

"Was Golda speaking Hebrew?"

"No, but she has a thick accent, which is weird because she was from Milwaukee."

"I didn't know that."

"Of course, you didn't, and do you know why? Because you don't listen. But do you know who would listen..."

I jumped in before she could continue the running insult. "I know, I know! That Filipino boy you should have adopted."

"Correct, Melissa. Five points!"

Israel proved to be fascinating and wonderful, and even at that young age, I knew there was something special about the place. Most of the country, like most of the Middle East, is a desert. Or as my mother described it, "It's like Vegas, except without casinos, magicians, or Charo."

The first stop we made was at the Wailing Wall. If you've never been there it's...oh hell, google it. I'm a busy woman; I'm writing a book; I don't have time to teach everyone. (Oh God, I'm sounding like my mother.) Anyway, one of the traditions at the Wailing Wall is that you write a prayer for someone or something and stick the paper inside one of the openings between the stones in the wall. There are rabbis all over the place to help you, although, according to *mi madre*, "They're not really rabbis, Melissa; they're just extras from *Yentl*. You know Barbra doesn't like to pay the cast and crew on non-shooting days."

I wrote a prayer asking God to watch over my mother and father. My father wrote a prayer asking God to watch over me and my mother. And my mother wrote a prayer asking

God to cancel Phyllis Diller's month-long run at Caesars Palace and give it to her instead.

After the Wailing Wall, we went to Bethlehem, which is part of Jerusalem—sort of Jerusalem adjacent. What's interesting is that while most of Jerusalem (and Israel) are under Jewish control, Bethlehem is under Palestinian control. Which meant that when we got to Bethlehem, we had to go through a checkpoint with armed soldiers, and switch cars and drivers. What amazed us is that everyone from both sides got along great with one another. The soldiers and drivers talked and laughed; not what we had anticipated at all. My father was convinced that most people get along just fine if we can get the politicians and religious zealots out of the way. My mother believed that they were all getting along because she was famous and they were all fans of hers. (Note: My mother had never done a show in Bethlehem, and speaks neither Hebrew nor Arabic.)

We also went to the place where Jesus was supposedly born. What shocked me was how crowded it was. Jesus's birthplace was packed with tourists, all pushing and shoving to get a closer look...it was like Black Friday at Bergdorf's. I'm surprised no one came away with a cashmere sweater or a Birkin bag. If as many people followed Jesus's teachings as visited his birthplace, the world would be a lot nicer. (Don't you love it when I get philosophical? What, you don't? Well then, don't worry about it; it doesn't happen often. Most of the time, I've got the depth of a skillet.)

Jesus's birthplace is marked by blue-and-yellow tile and an eternal flame that strangely looks like the LA Rams uniform. Way different from the only other eternal flame I knew, which was JFK's eternal flame in Arlington Cemetery. No blue-and-yellow tile, just grass and trees. It's stately and serene. My mother once said of Kennedy's grave, "Melissa, if you listen closely, you can hear Jackie, kneeling there, thinking, 'Uggh...now I'm going to have to fuck an ugly Greek billionaire.'"

One of our final stops was the Dead Sea, famed for its saltwater and scrolls. As we sat on the banks of the sea, we started talking about the historical importance of the scrolls. My father pointed out that they contained portions of the Bible, including passages from the books of Numbers and Leviticus, and that the majority of the texts found were written in Hebrew.

"I wonder if Golda Meir could read it," harrumphed my mother sarcastically. I sensed she was getting annoyed that my father was a) telling the truth and b) holding my attention.

"Your father didn't tell you this, but the Dead Sea is very salty...one of the saltiest bodies of water in the world."

She then leaned down, took a tiny handful of the water, and drank it. "Oh my God, it's saltier than semen! Edgar, taste this, tell me if I'm wrong."

Before I could run away and either find another family to live with or join the circus, my mother got up and said, "Time to leave!"

As the three of us made our way back to the car, my mother yelled out and waved to all of the other visitors (whom she assumed were fans), "Shalom, everybody, shalom!

"Melissa, did you know that the word 'shalom' has three meanings? It means, 'hello,' 'goodbye,' and 'peace.' And that's 'peace' as in 'peace and quiet,' not as in 'piece of ass.'"

"Yes, Mom; I knew that."

"Really? Well, do you know of any word in English that has three meanings? Take your time—*bitch*. The word 'bitch' has three meanings: female dog, informal complaint, and Joan Collins.

"I have another announcement to make."

Ignoring my father's glare, she went on, "Change of plans. Instead of going home, tomorrow we're going to Egypt! Won't that be fun?"

Shalom, everybody, shalom.

Tit for Tut

After we finished desecrating Israel, we continued our family vacation in Egypt. The "boat ride" from Ashdod, Israel, to Alexandria, Egypt, isn't long—less than a day—yet the two countries are worlds apart. It's like the difference between working on network television or cable. Israel is like working on a network show; everything is better, most importantly the catering. Egypt is somewhere between basic cable and public access, where the catering is a vending machine and a water fountain. The birthplace of Jesus notwithstanding, the only thing that Egypt has over Israel is history. Which stands to reason, since Israel wasn't founded until 1948 and Egypt was around for decades BC (before cable...what'd you expect?).

The three-hour car ride from Alexandria to Cairo was an experience in itself. Driving through nothing but arid, dusty desert, we passed hundreds of people sitting on boxes or old televisions or card tables. They were all waving at our car as we drove by. "Edgar, Melissa, can you believe this? Even here, in Egypt, I have fans. They must've seen my last *Tonight Show* spot."

My mother looking for the flag to signal the cocktail waitress that we were thirsty.

My father gently put his hand on hers—not out of love, but to get her to stop waving—and said, "Sweetheart, they don't get NBC over here."

"Oh?" replied my disappointed yet annoyed mother. "Then these must be flea markets; look at all those boxes. Let's stop and buy something."

It was my turn. "Mom, they're not flea markets, either. They're not selling things out of those boxes; they're living in them. All these people are begging for food or money or whatever people in passing cars can give them."

My mother looked genuinely shocked, a look rarely seen, which then turned into one of saddened dismay at the plight of these poor people. Without missing a beat, she immediately reached into her purse and began tossing tins of Altoids out the window to the beggars lining the road.

"Mom, I know your heart is in the right place, but I don't think bad breath is a major concern for these people."

"That's all I have on me, Melissa, other than two tampons, a lipstick, and a couple of buffet coupons from Caesars. And let's be honest, I need the tampons, these people aren't going to Atlantic City anytime soon, and the lipstick color is Fuck Me Red. If any of those women wear it, they'll get beheaded, which would not only be a human rights violation but also a terrible waste of a good lipstick."

While she may have been withholding her Maybelline, my mom's better side prevailed. She said to our driver, "Mustafah, when we get to our hotel, I want to make donations to help these people right away. Can you find the best way to do that?"

He didn't answer or even acknowledge that my mother was talking. At the time, I found that really rude of him, although in hindsight, I wished I had learned from him; it would have saved me years of stress, anxiety, low self-esteem, and Xanax.

"Mustafah? Can you help me with that?"

No reply.

So, she leaned forward and tapped him on the shoulder. "Mustafah, can you help me with that? Why are you ignoring me?"

"I'm not ignoring you, ma'am, I didn't know you were talking to me."

"Mustafah, how could you not know that I was talking to you?"

"Because my name is Bob."

Shockingly good to her word, as soon as we had checked into our hotel in Cairo, she and my father immediately reached out to the organizations and agencies that could help the poor, suffering "box people," as my mother referred to them.

After settling in and unpacking, we headed right back to the car to begin sightseeing. The city of Cairo was both modern yet ancient, beautiful yet horrifying. My mother couldn't believe how dirty and dusty it was. "I know Cairo is in the middle of a desert, but so is Las Vegas, and does Vegas look like *this*? No! Las Vegas is bright and shiny and filled with glitter and gold. Here, even the showgirls and hookers are dusty and ratty looking."

To which my father said, "Joan, those aren't showgirls or hookers; they're peasants."

"Really, Edgar? You don't think they'd hit their knees for a quickie if you offered them fifty drachmas? Peasants today, hookers tomorrow."

"Sweetheart, Egypt's currency is the pound, not the drachma."

"Oh shit! I forgot to exchange them at the border."

"Mom, where did you get drachma from?"

"I've had them since my European tour in 1967, before you were born."

"And you carry them with you, why?"

"Melissa, you never know when a huge drachma-only sale will crop up, and just like the Boy Scouts, I want to *be prepared*."

My mother continued, "It's way better than the other Boy Scout motto, 'Get your hands off my dick, Uncle Lou.'"

I said nothing because I wasn't completely sure what she was talking about. My father said nothing because he did.

"What's with the silence? Don't look at me like I said something awful. Think back...didn't either one of you find it odd that when your cousin Alan was a Boy Scout, he earned merit badges in knot tying and nipple torture?"

Driving through Cairo was an eye-opening experience on many levels. I was raised in Los Angeles, so I was used to crazy traffic, bad drivers, and oblivious pedestrians, but I wasn't used to pushcarts, goats, and camels sharing the road with cars. It was like a scene out of *Midnight Express* or *Lawrence of Arabia* or *Gandhi* (with food).

We were driving through the streets dodging people, animals, bicycles, and other cars. Zigzagging back and forth with clouds of dust everywhere. The roads didn't seem to have any lanes; everyone just drove where they fit—alleys, sidewalks, median strips, it made no difference. We were in the middle of an intersection when a camel crossed in front of us and stopped next to our car for no apparent reason.

"Mom, look, it's a camel!"

Without looking up from her *Vogue: Desert Issue*, she said, "No, it's not sweetheart. It's Mrs. Ginsberg from Temple Beth-Shalom, in Brentwood. I heard she was going on vacation the same time we were."

"No! It's a camel. Look at those humps."

My mother glanced out of the corner of her eye to look out the window and replied, "No, that's Mrs. Ginsberg. She had her breasts done in October. In my opinion, she had them made a little too big for her body. They look like the

San Onofre Nuclear Power Plant. And how she can go out without waxing is beyond me. She looks like a Yeti."

As the camel moved closer to the car, our driver, Bob, opened his window. The camel leaned in and Bob gave him some sugar cubes.

"Mustafah, what are you doing?"

"Giving this big camel some sugar cubes."

"Why, is he diabetic? Isn't some kind of juice better?"

"No, ma'am. No, ma'am, not diabetic. It shows them you're friendly and mean them no harm."

"Oh, I get it. They used to do the same thing with Orson Welles, except instead of sugar cubes, they gave him giant blocks of butter. It worked; he never bit anybody.

"And by the way, Melissa, I stand corrected; you're right, it's not Mrs. Ginsberg."

"Thank you."

"Check out those teeth. Doesn't he have a striking resemblance to Freddie Mercury?"

At that point, the camel moved away, the light changed, and we were off to see the Great Pyramid of Giza.

I think Giza's a real town, but it's in the Cairo zip code—probably to drive up real estate prices.

The pyramids are actually up on a plateau, right at the very edge of the city. On one side of the street was shopping: Burger King, Record Runner, Ross Burka for Less. On the other side of the street was the Sphinx, and then beyond that, the pyramids. I'm pretty sure that someone on the zoning commission was on the take.

My father and I got out of the car to check out the Sphinx; my mother lagged behind to make a phone call. After a few minutes, she still had not joined us, so we went back to check on her. There she was, pacing around on the phone yelling at someone.

"Joan, Joan, what's the problem? Calm down, sweetheart."

"Calm down, Edgar? Calm down? I am furious. First of all, I can't get anybody on the phone who speaks English. It's like calling American Airlines to make a reservation and getting someone who is clearly in India. In a thick accent, you hear, 'Hello, this is Kathy, can I help?' 'Yes, *Kathy*,' it's me, Maharishi Subramaniam Rivers.'"

Gently taking the phone out of her hand and hanging up, my father said, "Joan, darling…who is it you're trying to call?"

"The entertainment director at the MGM Grand in Las Vegas."

As one, my father and I both said, "Why?"

"The Sphinx, that's why. Have you seen it? It looks exactly like the entrance to the MGM Grand. Exactly. These bastards stole the idea from the MGM. There's a copyright infringement lawsuit that needs to happen."

"Mom, why do you care? You're not working at the MGM."

"No, but if they sue and win, I'll be entitled to a nice percentage. You want braces to fix your teeth, don't you?"

My father walked over to the car to have a cigarette with Bob, leaving me alone with Litigious Lucy. (And you wonder why I have abandonment issues?)

"Mom, I honestly think the MGM stole the idea from the Egyptians, not the other way around. I did some research; the Sphinx was built in 2500 BCE and Las Vegas wasn't built until the 1950s."

She paused to process the information and then, out of nowhere, said, "BC*E*? What's the 'E' stand for?"

"I don't know; I didn't research that."

"Ha! Of course, you didn't. You know who would know what the 'E' stands for? Your brother Melvin, that's who."

Slightly ashamed, I walked over to the car, hoping to share a smoke with my dad.

We then walked over to the three giant Pyramids of Giza. They weren't very far, but it took us over an hour because of my mother. She was in heels.

Again, I know what you're thinking: why would any sane person wear high heels in the middle of the Sahara? I can answer that for you simply: *Sane* is the operative word in your query. Lawrence of Arabia wore sandals. Jesus wore sandals. Cleopatra wore sandals. My mother wore Manolos.

"Mom, hurry up, we don't want to miss the Pyramids!"

"Miss the Pyramids? They've probably been there since 2500 BC*EEEE*, Melissa; they're not going anywhere."

The pyramids were truly awe inspiring. When you realize they were built centuries before formal architecture or engineering were discovered, it blows your mind.

"Mom, did you know that there are actually 118 pyramids all over Egypt, but the three at Giza are the main attractions?"

"Mmmhmm."

"And did you know that even though they had no engineering in those days, these pyramids are waterproof, airtight, and the stones have never shifted?"

"Mmmhmm."

"And did you know that underneath the pyramids are tombs for the dead pharaohs, kings, and queens?"

"Edgar? Remind me to call the entertainment director at the Luxor Hotel. Look at these things. If we combine the Sphinx and the pyramids, I think we have a class action suit."

Although being ignored, I continued.

"Did you know that the pyramids are the only one of the Seven Wonders of the World still around?"

"Melissa, that's only true if you don't consider Dolly Parton's boobs."

The biggest pyramid, the Pyramid of Khufu, is open for the public to tour the underground catacombs. I wanted to go. My father said, "I can't go, Melissa; I'm claustrophobic."

This was news to me. "Mommy will take you."

To her credit, my mother was both fearless and daring, so, after convincing her to put her heels in her purse, in we went, down hundreds of feet underground. Since there are no elevators in the pyramids—duh—you have to descend backwards on giant ladders with tow ropes. "Melissa, why are you so impressed? This is how they had to load Shelley Winters into her trailer while filming *The Poseidon Adventure*."

When we got to the bottom, there were dozens of hallways and catacombs. They were lit with generators so we could see the various carvings on the wall, mostly pictures or symbols. "Melissa, look over here! It says, 'Julio sucks.'"

The most noticeable thing about the underground city was how small everything was. Very tight rooms, and extremely low ceilings. Our tour guide told us that was because humans were much smaller centuries ago, about half the size of present average heights.

"Thank you for that information, Mustafah."

The tour guide asked, "How did you know my name was Mustafah?"

"My driver told me. Anyway, Melissa, Mustafah's absolutely right. Do you remember the trip we took to Philadelphia two years ago to see Independence Hall, the Liberty Bell, and Betsy Ross's house?"

I nodded as she continued. "Remember how we commented how small everything was? Back then, I thought Betsy was freakishly petite and supplemented her sewing business by doing some part-time carnival work, but no! It turns out everyone was small in those days.

"It also explains why George Washington's wooden teeth were so tiny. By the way, did you know that George Washington's teeth were actually made out of Scrabble tiles? When he smiled, his molars spelled out, 'Blow Me.' Thirty-seven points."

Fortunately, we now had to climb back up the ladder to go out. When we got to the top, my father was waiting for us.

"How was it?"

"Dad, it was really cool. I'll tell you all about it."

"Edgar, it's small, but it has good bones; a little bit of work and we could flip it for twice what it's worth. We should look into that. And Melissa, if you think Betsy Ross was small, wait till you see King Tut! Bob, take us to Tut!"

So we went back to Cairo, to the famed Cairo Museum. I can tell you, in all honesty, it was (and still is) one of the world's great museums. I could have spent days there, but my mother only wanted to stay as long as the gift shop was open. We were lucky that King Tut had finished his world tour and was back on display in Cairo at the same time we were there.

"Edgar, how is it that King Tut has been dead for thousands of years and he has more bookings than I do? Who's his agent?"

King Tut is buried in a small coffin with a partial glass top, so you can see his face. It's larger than a child's coffin, but smaller than a complete Easy-Bake Oven set.

The curator was telling us the complete history of Egyptian life during that period, but all my mother cared about was how good Tut looked. I must admit, he did look good, as if he had just died last week.

"Tut looks fabulous! Edgar, find out who did his work; see if he has an office in Beverly Hills. You know, Melissa, I did some research too, which is why I'm amazed at how cute he is. In reality, he had scoliosis, a cleft palate, buck teeth, fucked up toes, and malaria. Not exactly a looker. Whichever doctors got their hands on him had some amazing plastic surgery skills, I'll tell you that—and, as I mentioned before, look how small he is."

"I know, Mom, but remember he also died young. King Tut took the throne when he was only eight or nine years old. Maybe that's why he was so small."

"Actually, no, Missy. It's his mother, Nefertiti's, fault. She refused to breastfeed him because she didn't want to have saggy boobs that the other queens would make fun of when she went to the beauty parlor on spa day.

"So, he was malnourished?"

"Exactly! Nefertiti wouldn't let him suckle her nefertitties. So, he was small and sickly and weak. No tit for Tut.

"Edgar, all this food talk is making me hungry. I'm famished. Melissa, have you seen enough? Good. Let's go to the car. Do you think room service has matzo ball soup? Or maybe a pastrami on rye? Or maybe brisket, lean?"

As we headed to the car, I thought about telling Mom there probably weren't too many Jewish delis in Cairo, but decided to leave that job to Mustafah—I mean, Bob.

My mother was desperately trying to figure out which doctor botched the nose job.

The First Thanksgiving

Thanksgiving was my mother's favorite holiday. Mostly because it didn't require gift giving, which meant it was both fun *and* cost efficient at the same time. But also because it gave people a chance to get together over dinner and pretend to give a shit about what the other people at the table were saying.

After my father died, my mother immediately sold our house in Los Angeles (my childhood home)—without even letting me know it was on the market—and moved back to New York City to start her life over. (Imagine my surprise when I came home one day, my key didn't work, and the new owners threatened to call the police if I didn't stop trespassing.) Whether it was due to guilt, or fear of having to spend a holiday alone with me after not telling me about her "relocation," she began hosting Thanksgiving dinners at her townhouse in Manhattan. The first year, she invited friends who had nowhere else to go: you know, widows, divorcees, the terminally unfuckable, and whatnot. Then she began inviting relatives, business acquaintances, and rich neighbors who might leave her something when they died. Within a few years, it had turned into an iconic, Page Six, New York City "event," complete with butlers, maids, and catering. (Lest you think such spending might offset her aforementioned savings, please note that most of her guests were elderly, gay, or bulimic; two boxes of stuffing and a twelve-pound Butterball could feed the entire party and leave enough leftovers to feed the most upscale homeless people who, of course, live on the Upper East Side—just because you're homeless doesn't mean you don't know a nice neighborhood when you see one.)

When I was in the third grade, one of my school projects was to give a report on the story of the first Thanksgiving. And since I had no interest in actually researching the story (remember this was pre-Google), I asked my mother to tell me the tale. (Truth be told, I didn't really have to *ask* her...I simply shuffled into her bedroom with teary eyes and quivering lips, holding a pen and a blank notepad, and faster than you can say, "Pinocchio," she realized that this was a perfect opportunity for her to tell me a story.)

"Missy, darling, go sit over there on the guest chair and pretend it's my lap. Make yourself comfy and I'll tell you the story of the first Thanksgiving.

"It all started when the Pilgrims wanted to leave England because the food was lousy, the climate sucked, and the water had no fluoridation, so everyone had horrible teeth. And let's be honest, even way back then, no one wanted to make out with Bucktooth Billy or Gladys Greengums. So, a hundred or so disgruntled, horny people—they called themselves "Separatists" because they liked wearing separates instead of matching suits or jumpers—got on a boat to come to America. The boat was called the *Mayflower*, and it was like a Carnival Cruise ship with better plumbing. The *Mayflower* had a lot of amenities: miniature golf, yoga classes, Simple Simon on the promenade deck—they even had makeup seminars, which is how they came up with the Mayflower Compact.

"When they left England for America, the Pilgrims were heading towards Virginia because they heard it was on the water and that the weather was nice, sort of like Boca with seasons. But the *Mayflower* got lost and wound up in Massachusetts, which is *also* on the water, but the weather is not so nice, kind of like the panhandle."

Like a fool, I asked, "Mom, how did that happen? How did they get lost? Didn't they have a sextant?" (Yes, even at that young age, I knew what a sextant was. I don't know how I knew...I think it was from watching a lot of *Flipper* reruns on TV.)

"Yes, Melissa, they did. But they also had a Jewish navigator, Jacques Cousteauwitz. Jacques, who had no sense of direction, accidentally spilled coffee on his sextant and wound up veering off course. His wife repeatedly begged him to pull over and ask for directions, but every time she did, he'd snap at her, 'For God's sake, Miriam, I know where I'm going!'

"Needless to say, Missy, he didn't, and the Pilgrims wound up in Provincetown, Massachusetts...but in the off-season, when all the gays were in Key West, and the only people in town wearing feathers were the Indians. Also, since it was winter, the only place in town that was open was a wood-paneled lesbian bar called the Plymouth Rock.

"At first, the Native Americans were kind of welcoming, you know, a sort of *mi teepee es su teepee* kind of thing. They chatted, they played lawn darts, even a little volley-ball. One of the chiefs, Squanto, whose Hebrew name was Sitting Shiva, decided to invite the Pilgrims to dinner. Two of the Pilgrim leaders, Myles Standish, and his Black half-brother, Miles Long, accepted the invitation and showed up with their entourage—fashionably late—for what was to become known as the first Thanksgiving dinner.

"So far, so good, right? Wrong! On the invitation, Mrs. Squanto carefully carved the words 'casual attire,' loin-cloths, moccasins, beads. The Pilgrims clearly had a different understanding of what 'casual attire' meant in the new world. They arrived in formal wear—black and white outfits, with matching gloves and buckle shoes. I could've lived without the bonnets, but who knows, maybe all the girls were having bad hair days.

"Anyway, the Native Americans were clearly rusty at hosting; not since Columbus had they had any unexpected guests for a sit-down meal—they preferred buffet. The seating plan was a mess, there were no chairs, no stools, just rocks and stumps; not an accent pillow or a fun throw in sight. But they could be excused; they were new at this. Be honest, how often does a boatload of white people show up uninvited? The Pilgrims had no such excuse—they were just shitty guests. First, they showed up empty-handed. Then they complained about the food mostly because there was no vegan option—Jacques Cousteauwitz, his wife Miriam, and their daughters, Rivka and Ruchel, were all trying to adopt a plant-based burger. *And* instead of turkey, they served deer. Deer! Who ever heard of venison with stuffing and candied yams?

"To make matters worse, one of the Pilgrim matrons decided to rearrange the place cards. She said to Mrs. Squanto's daughter-in-law, Monica, 'Darling, I'd be more than happy to help you with your seating plan, because what you have created is a disaster. Everyone knows that you never seat a breast-feeding squaw next to a captain. And a papoose at the table...please!'

"Anyway, long story short, after dessert, the Native Americans, having had it up to their headdresses with the Pilgrims' boorish behavior, sent them home without either parting gifts, personalized dream catchers, or leftovers. The Pilgrims took this social *faux pas* as an insult and were so incensed, they drove them off their own land.

"The Native Americans moved to a town called Narra-gansett (which even they couldn't spell properly), which they selfishly named for themselves. The Pilgrims took over Cape Cod and began churning butter and churning out lots of thin, pasty-faced, white babies. Except for Rivka, whose children were darker and had thick, Semitic thighs and ankles. Ruchel never had children, but she made lots of "friends" at Plymouth Rock (Taco Tuesdays!).

"And that, Melissa, is the story of the first Thanksgiving."

FYI, when I presented my report to my fifth-grade class, the teacher gave me a "C." She said it was very interesting, but "factually challenged."

No One Likes Pushy

When I was young and single—and by "young," I mean nine—my mother started me on my journey to find the perfect man. (As I got older and remained single—or became single again—her standards dropped in direct proportion to her desperation to marry me off. At first, it was the search for the perfect man...then it became the imperfect man...then, a few years later, it was, "I didn't even notice the limp," and finally it got to, "Anything with a penis and a bank account.") Had I been a lesbian, I'm sure she would have embarked on a search to find me the perfect mannish woman.

I know what you're thinking...isn't nine a little young to start worrying about men? For most normal people, yes, but my mother wasn't normal.

Years later, my mother and I were in New York during Fashion Week, having lunch at Sarabeth's on W. 57th Street, when a couple of soccer moms came in with their daughters and sat at the table next to us. While I wasn't eavesdropping, I couldn't help but overhear their conversation...they talked about soccer, and dolls and homework...not once did the topics of boys, men, dating, marriage, or prenups ever come up.

For some reason, I flashed back to when I was that age. I asked my mother why she tried "hooking me up" when I was only in the fourth grade. She said, "Sweetheart, you can never start too soon. When we came to this country at the turn of the century, children were still dying of the bubonic plague, and since us kids were needed as workers, families had as many children as they could, and had them start their families as soon as possible. I was simply tending to the herd."

I said, "Really? For starters, you were born in Brooklyn, Grandpa was a doctor, you had one sibling, and you lived in a mansion in Larchmont. Not only that, you were born in 1933; the bubonic plague took place in 1350. How stupid do you think I am?"

I had barely finished the sentence when she snapped, "Well, Melissa, with that kind of attitude, you'll never find a man." She slammed her toast point on the table and told me that men don't like being corrected and really don't like pushy women. No one likes a know-it-all, especially me, but that's a separate conversation.

"Remember Susan B. Anthony? *Very* pushy and *very* alone. Never got married. She may have her face on a silver dollar, but she never had a man's face on her crotch. Yes, she was a dog, but still, a little nicey-nice might've gotten her a fella. And what about Mother Teresa? Famous, famous, famous and single, single, single."

I said, "She was a *nun*."

"Maybe. Or, perhaps, she became a nun because she was getting none. Or maybe she just washed the feet of the poor because she had a fetish. You don't know, you've never been to Calcutta. And even if it wasn't a fetish, what kind of a date was she? Who wants to dress up to wash peasants' feet?

"You want to meet Mr. Right, follow the lead of Mary Todd Lincoln. She knew when to shut up and give in. The night she and Abe went to the Ford Theater, Mary had no interest in going. She was tired, she was bloated, and was in no mood for a two-act with an intermission. But Abe insisted.

'Let's see a play, let's see a play.'

'C'mon, Abe,' Mary says, 'I don't feel like schlepping. What's wrong with the movies?'

'I know,' he says, 'but we can go to the movies anytime. Theater is special. It's a live event. Besides, you *know* I'm a Broadway Baby.'"

"Mom, there weren't movies back then; it wasn't a choice."

"Melissa, what did I just say about no one likes to be corrected? Are you even listening?

"Continuing on, Mary said to Abe, 'Yes, dear, I know. I remember the first time you went to free the slaves; they were all on the plantation working in the hot sun. And to help make the long, grueling day go faster, they sang spirited yet discordant Sondheim songs. And rather than freeing them, or joining them in the fields, you switched gears and burst into a rousing chorus of Jerry Herman's, "I Am What I Am."'

"So Abe starts whining and puts on his pouty face, so Mary gives in and they go to the theater. Three hours later, bang-bang, show's over and so is Abe. The rest is history."

I said, "Ma, how is that good? Mary gave in, 'knew her place'...and Abe got shot?"

"That's right, Melissa. Abe got shot."

"Mom, I'm missing your point. How is any of this good?"

"Simple. After an appropriate time of mourning (twenty minutes), Mary Todd was free to marry her *second* husband, Dr. Alan Weinstock, a urologist from Alexandria, who had two houses, a boat, a nice portfolio, and a small nose. And while slaves were no longer fashionable, he made sure she had live-in help. So, if you don't want to believe me, fine. Believe Mary Todd; that girl knew what she was doing."

I was speechless.

The soccer moms moved to another table.

True Love

As time moved on and I got older, it became harder for my mother to lie to me or tell me false stories...or at least lie to me about things that could be easily researched or disproven. Not that she didn't still lie, she did; she just had to become craftier about it. At one point, my mother discovered modern technology: Twitter, Facebook, Google, Myspace, Instagram, Grindr, and, believe it or not, Christian Mingle. She figured out a way to use these tech tools to help spread her falsehoods with joyful abandon.

My mother also used these platforms for Operation Fabrication Outreach...and by that, I mean she knew her fibbing days with me were coming to an end, so she had to find a way to share her "knowledge" with the world. And the only person that mattered in her world was *her* grandson, my son, Cooper. My mom *loved* Cooper; more than she loved me, more than she loved my father, even more than she loved her personal shopper at Bergdorf's, who gave her deep discounts even on non-sale items.

My mother used these grandma-grandson vacations with Cooper not just to bond with Cooper, but also to "teach" him about the history and goings-on of the world he lives in. Or at least her version of the history and goings-on of the world she thought he lived in.

When Cooper started becoming interested in girls, my mother took it upon herself to give him some unsolicited (and, according to Cooper, unwanted) advice on love and relationships, and especially on how men should treat women. So, she did what any loving, doting, delusional grandmother would do: She created a false Facebook account for Eva Braun and used it as an example of how a relationship can change in the blink of an eye. She sent him an email with a link:

> Cooper,
>
> Here's the link to Eva Braun's Facebook thread on the day she married Hitler. While the flash wedding was a nice surprise, the honeymoon turned out to be a hot mess. Also, don't forget this is just between the two of us; don't share this with you know who.
>
> *XO*
>
> *Nana*
>
> www.adolfandevaweddingregistry.org

FYI, I only know about this email because I accidentally came upon it when I was ~~breaking into Cooper's social media account~~ organizing Cooper's room.

TRUE LOVE

E. BRAUN

'Dolfy and I just tied the knot. Can't believe I'm finally "Frau H!" All's Reich in the world!!!

Congrats to you and Mein Fuhrer. May you both live as long as the Third Reich. Question: Is it true you're registered at Bed, Bombs, and Beyond?

H. GOERING

E. BRAUN

LOL. You kill me...along with six million others ☺ Your FB photo in ¾ profile really brings out your eyes. If I wasn't already spoken for...

You flatter me, you, anti-Semitic minx! You and AH look soooo happy in that pic.

H. GOERING

E. BRAUN

Our wedding night will be very special. Can't wait!!

I know what the plans are ☺ Adolf told me. VERY special. Eva, I know you hate surprises, so all I'm going to say is, "Don't eat anything spicy and bring a pillow."

J. GOEBBELS

I can't believe he told you but not me. I hate when he does that. Same as the Beer Hall Putsch and Kristallnacht. I say, "Al, where are you going?" And he flips me the bird and says, "Out." That's all; "out," like I'm some kind of piece of shit. And then I learn, AFTERTHEFACT that you and Rudy and everyone else knew but me. Arrggghhh. Joe, I'm me. I need to process.

E. BRAUN

K.

J. GOEBBELS

E. BRAUN

Just finished IM-ing with JG. I cannot believe Adolf thinks taking cyanide tablets and then having someone pour gasoline on us and set us on fire is very romantic. Who knew that when the pastor said, "...till death do you part?" he meant eleven o'clock?

Yeah, but think of how kewl you'll both look in your autopsy photos!

H. GOERING

E. BRAUN

What autopsy photos? We're going to be burned like schnitzels. *Auf wiedersehen.*

LIAR

AESOP

Dear Melissa,

You remember Aesop, the Greek fable guy? He wrote "The Tortoise and the Hare," "The Boy Who Cried Wolf," "The Goose that Laid the Golden Egg," and, of course, my favorite, "The Slovenian Model and the Corrupt, Orange Crazyperson." Or did he? (Wanna have fun? Read that last sentence out loud in the voice of Keith Morrison of NBC's Dateline. "It was a quiet Tuesday in a small, midwestern, American town until Joe Blow, a disgruntled former postal worker, senselessly killed an entire family of eight...or did he?")

I took time out of my busy ~~shopping~~, I mean, "work" schedule to do some exhaustive research about Aesop. And I discovered that Aesop the Storyteller may not have written any or all of those fables himself, and he may not have even been Greek. In fact, it's entirely possible that Aesop was actually a Jewish dry goods salesman from Queens named Morris Lituak, known in the garment industry as "The Zipper King of Flushing."

According to Aesop's IMDB page, he calls himself a "storyteller," not a fabulist or an auteur. And by the way, he has an IMDB page and I don't? Who the fuck is his publicist? I want a number! Anyway, Aesop may not have actually been a storyteller; there are rumors that he either stole a lot of other people's stories or bought naming rights and slapped his name on it for profit's sake. (Sound like anyone we know?) I got a lot of dirt on Aesop from a bunch of one-namers, Aristotle, Herodotus, and Plutarch, who were the Cher, Beyonce, and Madonna of their day.

According to Aristotle, "Ari" to his BFFs, Aesop was born in 620 BCE in the town of Thrace on the Black Sea. But Phaedrus, the big A's translator, said he was born in Phrygia. Yet others referred to him as "Aesop of Sardis" (not to be confused with David and Amy Sedaris, both acclaimed writers in their right) and "the sage of Lydia." Given all of this conflicting information, I believe he was either homeless, a grifter, or a homeless grifter.

Just like whether Harry is really Prince Charles's son, the question of whether Aesop actually wrote all of his fables is a matter of public debate. Some historians believe Aesop wrote a few of the fables, while many others believe he simply overheard shit, wrote it down, and put it out into the public. But everyone agrees that, over time, the fables changed. For example, "The Goose That Laid the Golden Egg," was originally titled, "The Goose Shit a Brick Because He Was on a High Fiber Diet." And the story of "The Tortoise and the Hare" was completely different. In what is believed to be the original version, the hare outran the tortoise by a mile, and when the tortoise finally crossed the finish line, the hare killed him and made turtle soup for everyone. When that ending didn't do well in focus groups, Aesop made changes and it became the "slow and steady wins the race" version we all know. By the way, just my opinion, but slow and steady doesn't win shit. When's the last time you saw the slowest guy in a race win? Usain Bolt didn't dawdle, and Michael Phelps didn't doggie-paddle; they ran and swam as fast as they could...which is why they won and won and won.

The only thing about Aesop that we know to be the absolute truth is that he was an ugly motherfucker. I'm not kidding; here's a quote from his Wikipedia page (and can you believe it? He has a Wikipedia page too):

The anonymously authored Aesop Romance begins with a vivid description of Aesop's appearance, saying he was "of loathsome aspect...potbellied, misshapen of head, snub-nosed, swarthy, dwarfish, bandy-legged, short-armed, squint-eyed, liver-lipped—a portentous monstrosity," or as another translation has it, "a faulty creation of Prometheus when half-asleep." The earliest text by a known author that refers to Aesop's appearance is Himerius in the 4th century, who says that Aesop "was laughed at and made fun of, not because of some of his tales but on account of his looks and the sound of his voice."

Sounds like his teen years were rough.

One other thing about Aesop that I know to be 100 percent true is that he was a playa', and if he had any money, he would have dated all of the hot supermodels of his time.

Till Death Do Us Part, Sort of

On June 16th, 2008, same-sex marriage became legal in California.

On June 17th, 2008, my mother became an ordained minister of the Universal Life Church, allowing her to preside over gay marriages.

On June 18th, 2008, she performed her first gay wedding.

On June 19th, 2008, she cashed her first check for doing it.

On our way out of the bank after a last-minute Monday-morning service, I said, "Mom, I'm sort of proud of you. You kinda did the right thing for some of the right reasons."

"Melissa, gay marriage is a wonderful thing," she replied. "Not just because it's the right thing to do, or that the Constitution guarantees equal protections under the law, but because I have such a big gay following, it opens up a whole new revenue stream for us. It'll be just like the red carpet—you can greet people coming in, and then you can toss it to me for the service. Think about it, there are tens of thousands of queens out there who can't wait to mince down the aisle. We could be making extra money fifty-two weeks a year. And not only that, gays have fabulous taste and are highly competitive; they're always trying to one-up their friends in giving the best swag. The swag alone is worth conducting the ceremony!"

In her 2014 Grammy-winning, *New York Times* bestseller *Diary of a Mad Diva*, my mother included the first draft of her remarks at a gay wedding she was conducting:

We are gathered here together to witness the exchanging of marriage vows between Lenny Goldberg and his furrier, Denny Glick. If there is anyone present today who knows of any reason why this couple should not be married—other than both sets of parents, thirty-seven states, most worldwide religions, and the offensive line of the Miami Dolphins—let them speak now or forever hold their peace.

Do you, Lenny, solemnly swear to take Denny to be your lawfully wedded, versatile bottom? Do you promise to love honor, cherish, and keep him for as long as you both shall live, or until he gets Alzheimer's and you can void the prenup and get everything in your name?

Do you, Denny, agree to the same stuff except that if things don't work out you get the cats and he gets the Lady Gaga CDs?

Denny, as a symbol of your promise to Lenny, please place the ruby slippers on his feet, click your heels three times, and say, "There's no place like homo, there's no place like homo, there's no place like homo."

Inasmuch as you have consented to the bonds of matrimony—not to mention tied to the bedposts with ball gags in your mouths—and you have exchanged your wedding vows before all those present today, by the powers vested in me by the state of New York, which I got free, online, I now pronounce you married. You may kiss...or better yet, spank the bride.

Say what you will, the woman had a flair for language. And a lot of what she said was actually true: she *did* have a huge gay following and gays *do* throw fabulous events. My mother loved the gay community. Not just because they became part of her fan base, but because, as she said to me one night, "Melissa, other than Warren Beatty in *Shampoo*, name one straight stylist that really knows how to do a woman's hair." I could not.

She couldn't understand homophobia. "What are people afraid of? That a gay burglar is going to break into their house, redecorate, and put up café curtains? It makes no sense.

"Gays are fabulous neighbors. Look at any gay neighborhood—gorgeous! Flowers, gardens, *tchotchkes*. You won't see any garbage on the front lawn or cars jacked up on blocks. In a gay neighborhood, the only thing you'll see jacked up on blocks is Jonathan's ass."

But I digress. My mother loved *all* marriages. She didn't necessarily believe that marriage had to be between "one man and one woman."

"Melissa, I don't care if a man marries a woman or a man or a sheep. As long as they're both happy."

"Mom, why would anyone marry a sheep?"

"Why? Why?" she screamed, as her knees buckled beneath her. "Good God, are you actually my child? What has happened to you? *Why?* Free sweaters, that's why!"

After taking a moment to get up off the floor and compose herself, she went on, "Wool can be pricey. You know, I'd never say never to the idea that I'd run off with a male sheep. Not just for the winter wear, but male sheep can weigh as much as four hundred pounds. Which means they can get cast on *The Biggest Loser*, and *I* could appear on the show as the concerned, yet nauseous, loving wife."

The horrifying part of what my mother had just said is not that she said it, but that it was entirely plausible she'd actually do it.[4]

She continued, "I don't think these 'one man, one woman' thinkers really thought that through. What if a man marries Siamese twins? Is that a marriage between a man and one-and-a-half women? Or what if a woman marries a little person or a giant? How do they classify that? I think that if two sentient beings are in love, that should be enough."

"Sentient beings? Mom? Really? When did you become Buddhist?"

"I didn't, but I read books by Ram Dass, the great spiritual leader. His first one was *Being Here Now*, and then, after he had a major stroke, he wrote *Still Here*."

"Didn't he die recently?"

"Yes. I think he should write a new book called, *Not Here Anymore*. You know, I'm always amazed by people who

---

[4] *Let's be honest; only for cashmere, not wool.*

accomplish great things after they've suffered debilitating illnesses. Like Ram, he had a stroke, but he kept on writing. Now, he may have had to hit the computer keys with his tongue, and he may have missed his deadline, but by God, the man wrote a book! Look at Beethoven; deaf as a post but wrote all that gorgeous music. And what about van Gogh? He only had the one ear, yet always managed to hear his wife Janice yell from the kitchen, 'Vinnie, don't forget to take your meds. You know how you get.'"

But as much as my mother loved the institution of marriage, she wasn't enamored with all of the rules. For example, she fought to have the words "To love, honor, and obey," changed to "Love, honor, and cherish." And by "fought," I mean at every wedding she attended, when the priest or rabbi said the word, "obey," she'd cough loudly while saying, "Bullshit" or, "Not a fucking chance." My mom was not a feminist, but as she explained it to me, "Missy, the only people I obey are the people who can write the checks or greenlight a series. I'm happy to cherish, adore—even blow—people who are higher up than me on the food chain, but obey? That's just for the big machers, cash cows, and Amex Black Card holders."

She also didn't believe that every marriage was meant to last forever, and that if a marriage ended, it didn't mean it was a failure; it meant that it lasted as long as it was supposed to. Or at least I think that's what she believed. Her actual words were, "This till death do us part thing is bullshit, unless you catch him cheating and kill him in his sleep because there's much less paperwork than divorce. And FYI, a pillow over the face, gentle pressure for six and a half minutes, should do the trick. No marks, no scars, no petechial hemorrhaging; it'll look like a grown man somehow died of sudden infant death syndrome. Tragic, but intriguing. Intriguing enough that you could probably sell the story to *Dateline* or *Forensic Files*, and turn lemons into lemonade. Not only that, you'd be a hot commodity—a grieving widow with money; husband number two will be right around the corner!"

To this day, I have no idea if she was serious or telling me the truth. She also wasn't done.

"My good friend, Elizabeth Taylor, was married eight times. Liz once said that if she loved a man enough to sleep with him, she loved him enough to marry him. If Madonna said that, she'd have been married to half of Europe.

"Elizabeth Taylor Hilton Wilding Todd Fisher Burton Burton Warner Fortensky. Her driver's license was three pages long. And with the exception of the last one, all of her husbands were rich and famous. The last one was the sidewalk sale husband, the one you meet when you're drunk and passed out on the casino floor and wake up the next morning in a cheap motel wearing nothing but a wedding ring and a horse collar.

"Elizabeth's first husband was Conrad Hilton Junior, who was known as Nicky. Why he was called Nicky, I don't know, but I heard it was because he liked to shave in the dark."

"Who did you hear that from? Anyone in particular, or are you making it up?"

"Melissa, how could you even think I would make something up? Of course, I heard it; I know people. Anyway, Nicky was the son of Conrad Hilton Senior, who was once married to Zsa Zsa Gabor. Did you know that? Of course not. Isn't this fun? It's like we're playing that game, Six Inches of Conrad Hilton. Zsa Zsa was married *nine* times. Combined, she and Liz were married seventeen times! Do you consider those failed marriages?"

"Well, I do ha—"

"Of course, you don't. Each marriage was supposed to last exactly as long as it did. And Zsa Zsa and Liz both did very well, I might add. Remember that gigantic diamond Richard Burton bought for Elizabeth Taylor? My God, that thing had a zip code. All I can say is that Elizabeth must've been really good in bed; she probably did so many Kegel exercises, her vag could probably suck Richard in from across the room.

"And Zsa Zsa, for a woman with absolutely no talent or skills, she lived like a fucking queen."

"I know, and I really don't understand it. When I was little, you, me, and Daddy used to watch Zsa Zsa Gabor as a guest on TV talk shows all the time. If she had no talent, why was she on TV?"

"Because she was a 'personality,' Melissa. For some inexplicable reason, people liked to see her. She was like the Kardashians, except without the black dick fetish. Which, by the way, *I* don't understand. I get it if one of the girls only liked Black men, but *all* of them, including the mother, Kris Jenner? That's very unusual. But I must say, I give Kris credit for diversity. She's dated Black men, was married to an Armenian man, and was then married to a woman-man. How hip is that? I'm surprised one of the daughters isn't married to a gay guy or a transgender person."

"Maybe the attraction to gay men isn't a hereditary trait?"

"Oh really? I can refute that in one word: Judy Garland and Liza Minnelli."

"That's five words."

"Oh Melissa, please; they're one person. I hate it when you get all judge-y. What I'm saying is that both Judy and her daughter Liza both had a couple of gay husbands on their resumes. I wonder if they knew? I mean, how did Liza not know that Peter Allen was gay? For their honeymoon, he took her to the Ramrod.

"But come to think of it, being married to a gay man might be fabulous. Think about it: they dress great, they smell great, they have disposable income, and you don't have to fuck them. What's not to like?"

Cut to: A few weeks later. My mother and I are in the waiting room at our Botox doctor's office. I'm going to have my frown line filled in; my mother's going to have the entire left side of her face filled in with low-fat cottage cheese.

"Mom, do you remember a few weeks ago, we talked about Elizabeth Taylor and Zsa Zsa Gabor having been married multiple times?

"I was just wondering why women get married so many times, but men don't."

"Because men cheat," she replied. "Women want meaningful relationships; men want a meaningful three minutes."

"Three minutes? Who's done in three minutes?"

"Kermit the Frog. We had a thing."

"You had a 'thing' with Kermit the Frog?"

"Yes. We met on the set of *The Muppets Take Manhattan*. You know, Melissa, on-set romances aren't that unusual. Someday, I'll tell you the backstage story of *The Bad News Bears*."

"But it only took three minutes?"

"Yes, but they were a memorable three minutes. You know, Missy, I should've married him; think of how long your legs would've been.

"But there are men who do get married a lot," she continued. "Like Larry King. He's been married eight times, and it's always the same story: he meets a beautiful woman, they get married. Then the woman gets Lasik surgery, regains her sight, and poof! They're divorced...

"Remember Henry the VIII? He was married *six* times, which in those days was unheard of. Two of the marriages were annulled and two of them ended when the wives were beheaded. Clearly, the man had some repressed anger issues."

"If marriages are so bad, why are you such a big fan?"

"Because, without women, Melissa, every conversation men have would be about some mundane bullshit, like carburetors or lawn care or the Knicks.

"So when I encourage you to get married, Melissa, I know what I'm talking about. I've prepared you for your marriages since the day you were born; as a baby, your first words were, 'I do.'

"Sweetheart, someday you'll thank me for all of this sage wisdom and personalized advice I've given to you. And I know you'll have the best nine or ten marriages a gal could ever have.

"Anyway, my love, I've got to run. I've got a date with a guy I met at the supermarket."

"Mom, seriously! You...were at a supermarket?"

LIARS

THE FOUR WHORESMEN OF THE APOCALYPSE

Dear Melissa,

Larry King. Zsa Zsa Gabor. Mickey Rooney. Elizabeth Taylor. Between them, they've been married thirty-three times, to thirty-one different people (there were a couple of repeat customers), but, thankfully, never to one another.

As you know, I hate gossiping about other people's marriages, but the four of them are such liars, I can't help myself. They're liars because of the vows they made, you know, "to love, honor, obey...cherish...richer or poorer...in sickness and in health...blahblahblah." Obviously, none of them made those vows truthfully—otherwise they wouldn't have been married thirty-three times.

Look, I understand that mistakes happen. So, had Zsa Zsa or Liz or Mickey or Larry been divorced once, maybe even twice, I'd say, "Fine. They tried their best; it just wasn't meant to be." But eight or nine times? At some point, you have to realize that you're just full of shit and the vows you took are about as important as the leftover catering is three days after the wedding.

As much as I hate the feminist thing—you know, "give me stuff because I have a vagina"—I'd like to point out the sexism thing going on in these marriages. Both Zsa Zsa and Liz were drop-dead gorgeous... both Mickey and Larry were drop-dead not. Seriously, Mickey Rooney was married to Ava Gardner. Ava Fucking Gardner! She was one of the most beautiful women INTHEWORLD and Mickey was sixty inches (five feet tall) of fun. Perhaps he had sixty inches somewhere else, which would explain the fun...and the reason Ava married him. And as for Liz, every man in the world, even the gay ones and the clergy, would love to have been with Elizabeth Taylor. Do you think every woman in the world felt the same way about Larry Fortensky?

To be fair, I have not seen the text of the thirty-three sets of marital vows each of them took, but I'm pretty certain they all had the same basic idea: be kind, loving, and supportive of one another, and don't fuck other people. Depending on whether or not the bride or groom is religious, sometimes the name of God, Jesus, Allah, or, if they're Jewish, Barbra Streisand, is included in the vow.

Speaking of Jewish, Larry King and Elizabeth Taylor were both Jewish; did you know that? Larry was born Jewish; his real name was Lawrence Harvey Zeiger. He changed it to "King" for show business purposes, because Zeiger sounded "too Jewish." Ironically, Jordan's King Hussein's real name was Murray Fishbein; he changed it for political purposes because Fishbein sounded "too Jewish." And Zsa Zsa Gabor's parents were of Jewish "heritage," which I think means they once got a good deal on a timeshare in Florida.

Elizabeth Taylor converted to Judaism in 1959, when she married Eddie Fisher, who was Jewish. Liz took her new religion seriously: she kept a Jewish home, became an avid supporter of Israel, and, rumor has it, once ate 435 potato latkes in less than fifteen minutes.

As everyone knows, when Elizabeth first hooked up with Eddie Fisher, he was already married—to Debbie Reynolds, Elizabeth's best friend. (I know, with friends like that...I don't have friends like that. If my BFF makes a pass at my BF? FU! I'm a simple, old-fashioned gal at heart.)

You may not know this, but Elizabeth Taylor was also in a weird triangle with Zsa Zsa Gabor. One of Zsa Zsa's husbands was the wealthy hotel baron, Conrad Hilton Sr. One of Elizabeth's husbands was his wealthy son, Conrad "Nicky" Hilton Jr. (Urban myth is that the son liked to be called "Nicky" so as not to confuse his wife or mother and have them accidentally start fucking the wrong Conrad Hilton.) In fairness to Liz, I doubt she was lying when she took her marital vows to Nicky Hilton. He was her first husband; how could she have known there would be oh so many more? Ditto for Zsa Zsa; Conrad Hilton Sr. was her second husband, so she, too, had not yet learned the fine art of breaking vows. But by the time she married her final husband, Prince von Whateverthefuckhisnameis, you'd think she'd have known she was lying, and instead of saying, "I do," could have just said, "Maybe."

The same goes for Larry and Mickey. Sort of. Ava Gardner was Mickey Rooney's first wife, and I'm sure he took his vows with her seriously. But I don't believe he took his vows with the other eight wives honestly. Because Mickey's marriage to Ava Gardner ended—after a year—when he cheated on her! If you look like him and can't be faithful to *her*, you can't be faithful to anyone.

Larry King was a diehard baseball fan and I think he married his wives accordingly—like a pitching staff: He had a starting rotation and would trade them every fifth day for a new pitcher. I can't swear that

Larry was lying when he said his "I do's" but I heard that his vows always included the closing phrase, "...till Wednesday do us part."

My point in all this is to take your marriage vows seriously...or don't take them. Even if you're one of those earthy, vegan assholes who likes to write their own vows, you get to determine what you're agreeing to. So, keeping your word shouldn't be that difficult.

I personally have no such worries; for starters, no man wants me. No reasonable person with a penis and a pulse is saying, "Hey, I gotta get me a piece of that old thing." Plus, I have no plans or intentions of ever getting married again. I've done that twice. The only way I'll get married again is if a blind zillionaire with serious health issues and no dependents pops the question. (The question, of course, is, "Joan, is it okay if I leave everything to you?") I still go out, but my hidden mantra is: "I will like you, have fun with you, maybe fall in love with you, but never marry you, never live with you, and never give you the passwords to my computer, cell phone, or bank card." Works for me.

And that's the truth.

Death Be Not Shroud

My mother loved funerals, and I mean loved. She lived for them. To paraphrase Elizabeth Barrett Browning, "How do I love funerals? Let me count the ways." For starters, my mother was thrilled that everyone wore black. (When she said, "Once you go black, you never go back," she was talking about fashion, not fucking.)

Or should I say, almost everyone. Once, after seeing a widow in navy blue, my mother clutched her pearls, and said, "Melissa, if you see someone at a funeral wearing bright colors, they're trying to draw attention to themselves. How stupid are they? You don't need to wear bright colors at a funeral to draw attention to yourself; that's why God invented large diamond brooches and jewel-length sleeves."

My mother was also very into funeral food (even though she herself lived on a diet of Altoids and M&M's with the occasional Milk Dud); she told me she sometimes decided on whether or not to even attend a funeral totally based on the post-cemetery menu. For example, my mother rarely attended an Irish wake because she hated corned beef, and cabbage is very gassy. "Missy, as you know, 'empathy' is my middle name, but a room of relatives farting would bring tears to my eyes, and not because I'm sad."

Conversely, she enjoyed funerals at ethnic churches because, "Good food, great music; let me tell you—even in grief, they really know how to throw a funeral."

Gay funerals were her favorites. "They're not sad, 'boo-hoo' events—they're more like soirées with great food, great décor, great gossip, and great clothes. Other than the stiff in the box bringing down the room, everyone has a great time."

Which is how it should be. A funeral should reflect the life of the person who died. One night, after binge watching three seasons of *Forensic Files* on Netflix, my mother said to me, "Melissa, all of these fabulous murders have me thinking about my death. Or, to be more precise, my funeral.

"Do you remember Catherine the Great, Russia's longest-reigning female ruler?"

"Of course, I do; she was the Oprah of her day."

"Really," my mother snapped. "Did she also have a bestie named Gayle? Do you know why Catherine was known as 'The Great?' Because she was great in bed, that's why. And even though Catherine was homely—behind her back they called her 'The Siberian Husky'—she got around. Turns out, Queen Cate started doing Kegel exercises the day she was born, and by the time she was twenty, her vag could do more tricks than David Copperfield. No man could satisfy her... which is why she started *shtupping* horses. Why horses, you ask? Because they're hung like horses, that's why. (Hence the saying, 'hung like a horse'; make sense now?) And as you know, she died while sowing her oats. An actual Italian stallion was being lowered onto her when the ropes broke and the horse crushed her. Talk about coming down the stretch. She went from being Catherine the Great to Catherine the Flat. She was like a fucking Colorform; she was the original Flat Stanley. Schoolchildren had to carry her around to interesting places and take photos of her as a class project."

Even though I could see that my mother was wound up, I foolishly decided to interject some truth. "Mom, the horse thing is just a myth, there's no proof of that."

"Really? Hmmm? Then why did she lie in state on a bale of hay? How come instead of burying her or cremating her, they turned her into a jar of glue? Why do you think 'Elmer's' was her safe word?

"You know who else was buried as they lived, Melissa? Elvis. Granted, his family had a tough choice—bury him as he lived, or as he died? Luckily, they chose lived; probably it wasn't a hard choice because he died on the toilet—sitting down, hunched over, with his pants at his ankles. I would have chosen that option because how appropriate was it that the King died on the throne?

"But they decided to bury him as he lived...a sweaty, bloated pill-head. Elvis was stuffed into a jumpsuit and then into a casket. They didn't even have room for the Prince Valiant cape. Thank God they found him before the postmortem bloating started. His coffin was lined with cotton rather than satin, and instead of a lid, the coffin had a childproof cap. Not only that, but just in case he had to be exhumed, it came with three refills."

I knew my mother was making all of this up (which is another nice way of saying "lying"), but I also sensed that this conversation was going somewhere.

"Sweetheart, I've written a little something about what I want for my funeral. And I'm putting it in my next book... Not that I don't trust you, I just want witnesses, like my fans who will turn on you if you don't carry out my wishes."

Here is my mother's last request from her book, *I Hate Everyone...Starting with Me*:

When I die (and yes, Melissa, that day will come; and yes, Melissa, everything's in your name), I want my funeral to be a big show biz affair with lights, camera, action...

I want craft services, I want paparazzi, and I want publicists making a scene! I want it to be Hollywood all the way. I don't want some rabbi rambling on; I want Meryl Streep crying in five different accents.

I don't want a eulogy; I want Bobby Vinton to pick up my head and sing "Mr. Lonely." I want to look gorgeous, better dead than alive. I want to be buried in a Valentino gown and I want Harry Winston to make me a toe tag. And I want a wind machine so that even in the casket my hair is blowing just like Beyoncé's.

Clearly, my mom wanted her funeral to reflect the way she *lived* and, when she died, and as I've said in the past, I honored that request as best I could. Even though her funeral was in New York City, it was Hollywood all the way: celebrities, cameras, velvet ropes, and helicopters overhead. The only things missing were the wind machine (the fire department said because there was so much silicone, collagen, and Botox in the room, one brief spark could set the whole synagogue ablaze...) and Meryl Streep—who said she was busy making *Mamma Mia III* (which takes place in a nursing home where Bjorn and Agnetha wet themselves when they sing, "Waterloo"). Oh, and I had to return the diamond toe tag because, as I'm sure you know, Harry Winston only *lends* his jewelry to celebrities; nothing is for keeps.

As for me, when I die, hopefully a long time from now, I don't want a big, fancy funeral or a memorial service. (Trust me, there's no money left after my mother's big, fancy send-off.) I want to be cremated and have my ashes put into an electronic ankle bracelet that Cooper will have to wear (if he wants his inheritance), just so I can annoy *him* for the rest of *his* life. It's a Rivers family tradition.

The Less the Merrier

In the early 2000s, I was visiting my mother in New York. Around midnight, I went upstairs to say goodnight to her. I found her in her bedroom, sitting in her favorite chair, rocking back and forth, cradling her Daytime Emmy Award like a baby, so I said, "Mom, what are you doing?"

She said, "Putting the baby to bed."

I said, "Have you lost your mind? What are you going to do next, burp the fucking thing?"

She said, "Melissa, other than hosting *The Tonight Show*, appearing on Broadway, having my own talk show, going to White House dinners, becoming friends with the Royal Family, and having a fashion line on QVC, you're the best thing that's ever happened to me. Have I ever told you that I always wanted more children but never had them?"

"Why not?" I foolishly asked, wishing I could suck the words back in as they left my mouth.

My mother took a long pause and got that "here comes the bullshit" look on her face, and said, "It wouldn't have been fair to the baby. I was on the road all the time, going to

Las Vegas for weeks on end, writing movies, and appearing in plays."

"You did all that when *I* was a baby!"

"Yes, and I regret it a little. Even though you were the only seven-year-old who knew how to double down on a pair of nines, I still wish I'd given you brothers and sisters—or, as your father thought of them, deductions."

Then she put Baby Emmy on the nightstand and began dabbing her eyes to dry the crocodile tears she'd learned to cry when she was in acting school in the sixties. After a minute or so, and no response from me, she realized I wasn't buying it, so she took another tack.

"Melissa, the truth is...women with lots of children are never happy. Look at Mia Farrow...she has fourteen hundred children of all different races, sizes, and genders...some she gave birth to, some she adopted, and a couple she *allegedly* stole from shopping carts in Target when their real mothers were pulling boxes of extra-large Spanx off of the top shelves.... The point is, Mia is not happy. When is the last time you saw her in a feel-good movie, like *Rosemary's Baby*? Never. That's when."

"Mom, I don't think Mia's unhappy because she has lots of children. I think she's unhappy because Woody Allen married one of them."

"Who, Soon Yi? Don't be ridiculous...Mia had plenty of other kids to replace her...what's the boy's name, you know, the one that looks like Sinatra...Ronan? Anyway, forget Mia. What about The Old Woman Who Lived in a Shoe? *She* had so many children she didn't know what to do. So you know what she did? She took up day drinking. And who could blame her? Not only did she have lots of children, but the shoe was a flat! Not a boot, not a thigh-high, didn't even have a peep-toe; I'm surprised those kids didn't suffocate. Talk about unhappy."

"That's just not true, Ma. There are plenty of women who have lots of kids and are very happy. Like Angelina Jolie."

"She doesn't count; I'd be happy if I looked like that too."

"Okay, Mom, what about the Brady Bunch? In fact, it turns out the father was more than happy; he was gay! Plus, they had that fabulous housekeeper, Alice, who worked 24/7 and never stole anything. If I could find good help like that, I'd be happy. And what about Mrs. Duggar? She has nine-teen children—and counting—and she's always smiling."

"She's smiling because the husband finally got off of her for five fucking minutes. My God, the poor woman barely had time to flush the afterbirth before Jim Bob was locked, loaded, and ready to go again. Even worse, her vagina's the size of the Grand Canyon. She could make extra money having burros give tourists rides up and down the sides. Mrs. D's vag must be stretched more than Donald Trump's waist-band. And the labia? Oh please; when she opens her legs, she looks like Jocelyn Wildenstein, smiling."

And, at that moment, I realized why I was (technically) an only child; it had nothing to do with Las Vegas or Mia Farrow or The Old Woman Who Lived in a Shoe...my mother simply didn't want stretch marks or a stretched vajajay.

"Finally, I get it! You thought it was more important for *you* to have a tight hoo-ha than for *me* to have a brother or sister."

"Okay, yes, Melissa, yes! You're right; I didn't have more children because I didn't want to be all stretched out. You know what they say, 'loose lips sink ships.'"

Having finally gotten at least some of the truth out of her, I paused, took a breath, and asked, "Then why didn't you just adopt a brother or sister for me?"

"Melissa, I didn't have to adopt a sister for you; I won one."

She picked Emmy back up, gave it a kiss, and resumed rocking back and forth. I went downstairs to have a cocktail and call my therapist.

Bright Lights and Hollywood!
Part 1

I can't tell you how many times, when being interviewed, I've been asked, "Melissa, did you *want* to be in show business or did your parents drag you in?" (Actually, I probably *could* tell you, but I'd have to go back and watch/read/ listen to every interview I've ever given in my entire life, and between obsessing, isolating, and self-loathing, I simply don't have the time.)

Growing up, I wasn't sure what I wanted to be. I loved riding horses, but by age six, I weighed forty-two pounds and was already far heavier than most professional jockeys. (Little known fact: When Steve Cauthen rode Affirmed to the 1978 Triple Crown, Steve only weighed eleven pounds!) I thought about being an astronaut, but my mother dashed that dream pretty quickly. "Melissa, there are no bathrooms up there; how are you going to put on your makeup or shave your legs?"

I wasn't very good at math or science, so a lot of career opportunities were off the table, things like doctor, nurse, chemist, accountant, stockbroker, or banker. In fact, my math skills were so bad, I didn't even have a future as a cashier... even with electronic cash registers that told you how much change to give back. Had I been able to get past Mendel and his pea pods in my grasp of sequencing, I might have become an FBI profiler, which I would have loved. To this day, I am obsessed with TV shows about criminal profiling. I know I would've been damn good at it. Remember when Nicole Brown Simpson and Ron Goldman were murdered? (Of course, you do; that was one of those events whose enormity made it time immemorial, like 9/11 or Neil Armstrong's walk on the moon, or when Mira Sorvino won the Oscar and everyone knew it was a mistake.) Not two minutes after the news of the murders broke, I announced to all my friends and family that O. J. did it. My God-given profiling talents were on full display in that moment. "Listen up, everybody! Ron and Nicole were killed by an athletic Black man with big hands, amazing foot speed, a Heisman Trophy, and an ongoing national commercial contract with Hertz."

To which my mother said, "How do you know that, Melissa?"

I replied, "Who else could it have been, Steve Cauthen? Not likely, he weighs eleven pounds.

"O. J. had the means, the opportunity, and the time. And the motive. He targeted Ron Goldman because once, when Ron was O. J.'s waiter at Mezzaluna, he forgot to put O.J.'s salad dressing on the side. Nicole was simply in the wrong place at the wrong time."

Surprisingly, my mother smiled at me instead of scowling. I'm not sure if it was because of my creative storytelling or because I was lying, but either way, I appreciated the non-verbal support.

At the University of Pennsylvania, I majored in European history. Which qualifies me to be...wait for it...nothing, other than good to travel with and interesting at cocktail parties. Okay, I know what you're thinking: "Melissa, you could've been a professor and taught European history!" True, but why would I want to do that? The reasons I chose to study European history are a) I thought I might be able to get the university to send me on free trips to Europe, and b) I'd only have to know about things that had already happened, and not concern myself with things that might happen in the future. A degree in European history could also qualify me to be a historian, but let's be honest, it's not exactly a huge job market; there are only three historians that anybody's ever heard of: Michael Beschloss, Jon Meacham, and Doris Kearns Goodwin, and that's only because they're on MSNBC all the time. (Can I point out that Doris Kearns Goodwin has had some really good work done? Now if only she would straighten her wigs, she'd have her own series. Just sayin'.)

Which basically left me with two options: mortuary science or show business. I knew I couldn't be a mortician because I'm not a people person, so show biz was it for me.

Since I come from a show biz family (my father was a producer and my mother was a comic, actress, writer...and, if you take her word for it, singer, dancer, fluffer, third violin in the NY Philharmonic, and stunt double for Sophia Loren), it's kind of logical for me to enter the industry. For the Rosenberg/Rivers clan, entertainment is the family business, in the same way that making pianos is a family business for Steinway & Sons, or, for the Santini Brothers, moving furniture. The Gotti family business is putting people in the trunks of cars—occasionally, before they're dead (God is in the details). The Kardashian family business is...well, I don't actually know what it is, but they're making a fortune, so they must be good at it.

I'll never forget the first thing my mother told me about the entertainment industry: "Melissa, show business is one giant illusion. It's like magic; a good magician wants you to think what he's doing is real, when it's not.

"For example, do you think magicians are really sawing women in half? Of course, not, it's an illusion."

"It would be much more interesting if they did."

"Melissa! How could you say that?"

"I...I...I—"

"My God! You're brilliant! Imagine the crowds Ted Bundy would draw if he played Vegas? And as for his performance? He'd kill!

"Show biz is *all* fake. All of it. Think about it, Missy. Let's take acting, for starters. Acting is simply pretending you're someone else. It's basically playing make-believe with backlighting. Remember *The Wizard of Oz*? When you were a little girl, it was your second favorite movie, right behind *Deep Throat*."

"MOM! *Deep Throat* was not my favorite movie!"

A brief pause, then, "Oh, I'm sorry; I'm confusing you with your father. Your favorite childhood movie was *Judgment at Nuremberg*."

"No, Mom. It was *White Christmas*."

"That's right; I get them confused. One starred Spencer Tracy and was about the Nazis who were mean to the Jews, and the other starred Bing Crosby, who was mean to his children. Simple mistake."

"Mom, *White Christmas* wasn't about Nazis who were mean to Jews."

"It was in the subtext, Melissa. Anyway, my point is that, in *The Wizard of Oz*, the flying monkeys weren't really flying monkeys. They were a family of very hairy Mormons who enjoyed wearing tiny vests while soaring through the air with harnesses strapped to their magical underpants. They were *acting*. It wasn't real.

"In *Sophie's Choice*, surprise, surprise, those weren't really Meryl Streep's children; they were bulimic actors who were starved and sent out in the cold with wet heads so they'd look sickly. And the movie wasn't filmed at Auschwitz, it was filmed in Orlando at Disneyworld, in the It's a Small Camp After All exhibit.

"Remember *Dracula*? Do you think Bela Lugosi actually drank blood? Do you think he'd wander into a restaurant and ask, 'What plasma do you recommend with fish?' Bela was vegan, for fuck's sake.

"Even *101 Dalmatians* was fake. There weren't one hundred and one dalmatians; there were four Samoyeds with bad skin and a high-speed camera. But you *thought* it was one hundred and one dalmatians, which was the whole point of it."

I realized she could go on like this for hours, so I jumped backed in and said, "Were you Cruella de Vil?"

Without missing a beat, my mother laughed a disturbing laugh and sighed, "Oh, Melissa, you are too funny. Let's play a game, shall we? It's called Guess Who's Not in Mommy's Will? Ding-ding, the answer is 'Melissa.' You win!

"Next, let's talk hair and makeup. Again, creating an illusion. Do you remember how upset you got watching *The Sound of Music* when you found out that Julie Andrews actually had short blond hair and not the beautiful brunette upsweep she sported in *Mary Poppins*? You cried for two hours when you realized that Julie's brown hair was a wig. And you cried for another two when you realized she didn't actually sleep with Christopher Plummer. I can understand that, though; Plummy was a peach in the sack.

"And can we discuss Edward James Olmos?"

"Edward James Olmos has makeup people? Jeez, they're doing a terrible job."

"No, Melissa, they're doing a fantastic job. In real life, Big Ed has perfect skin—alabaster white and smooth as a baby's behind. But there are a million guys in Hollywood like that, so Big Ed created a niche for himself—the strong, yet kind-hearted Latin man, an antihero with pockmarks. Before every scene, he's spray-painted with a sticky beige goo, and then the prop-master gets a machine gun and shoots chick-peas at his face for forty-five minutes. You laugh, but without his makeup team, Big Ed is just another fair-haired farm boy from Iowa."

I was flabbergasted. I didn't know where to begin. So much bullshit, so little time. All I could say was, "Why do you call him Big Ed...you know what? Don't tell me. I don't want to know."

"And it's not just movies or TV series or Broadway shows, which I'll get to..."

"Please God, no."

"...Commercials! They're nothing more than thirty-second lies. How many women do you know who make loud, terrifying, orgasmic screams when they find a laundry detergent that works on greasy, grimy dirt? When is the last time you actually saw a dog that could not only talk, but do so while driving a sporty, new Honda Civic?

"And Broadway theater? *Everything* is fake, starting with the fact that not one single male cast member is straight. They're all gay; in fact, they all have riders in their contracts that say the dressing room snacks will not add any weight to their hips."

"Mom, Richard Burton has starred on Broadway; so has Dustin Hoffman, Jack Lemmon, James Earl Jones...are you saying that *all*..."

"No, no, I'm not. I'm just saying that one hundred percent of the men on Broadway are gay. Remember when we saw *Equus*, with Richard Burton?"

"Well, of course I do; it was a little aggressive to take a kindergartener to."

"Right. But didn't you notice that Richard and the horse were extremely close? And by extremely close, I mean *uncomfortably close*. There was definitely a chemistry between them. I don't care how much technique an actor has, love is love *is love*.[5]

"Mom? Even if what you're saying is true, which I doubt, it doesn't make Richard Burton gay."

"The horse was male. His name was Dave."

"Oh, well then, I stand corrected. Makes perfect sense." I began rolling my eyes with such vigor, my mother thought I was having a seizure.

"Oh my God, Missy. Don't swallow your tongue! Hang on, hang on!"

Needless to say, I wasn't having a seizure. I was just stunned by the commitment my mother made to her bullshit story. She began furiously rummaging through her purse.

"Melissa, I may have to run and find something to put between your teeth, because all I have in my bag is a Lanvin number seven eyebrow pencil, and it's very expensive, so I'll have to keep looking. Don't die while I'm gone."

"Mom! I'm fine. A little shocked but fine."

"Oh, I am so relieved. The thought of wasting good eyebrow pencil is very upsetting. You see, sweetheart, *this* is why you belong in show business. Without even trying, you had me believing you were having a seizure. You were acting. And acting is lying!"

---

[5] Lin-Manuel Miranda said, "Love is love is love." It was a few years after my mother died; however, I say, "If *she* can lie, why can't I?"

"So, is that why you decided to call show business your career, so you could lie?"

"Melissa! Of course not. I didn't call show business, show business called me! How can I put this delicately? I was to the fucking manor born!"

Bright Lights and Hollywood!
Part 2

I remember back in the early '90s, when Andre Agassi broke into the world of professional tennis. He was a young, hip, hot shot, a rising star. He wore funky clothes and a headband and had wild, frosted blonde hair. He was outspoken in a fun way. He was exciting to watch and packed the stands with fans...long before he won anything. He was famous for—and got grief for—doing TV commercials with the tag line, "Image is everything." His fans loved it, but his critics hated it. His critics would respond with a "Why don't you win something before you open your big yap?" mentality. To prove them wrong, he did just that. Agassi won seven Grand Slams and his image went from being a youthful loudmouth to being a respected elder statesman. And he also revealed that he only wore a headband to keep his toupee in place. Toupee! I was shocked.

Turns out Andre began losing his hair at an early age and was so concerned with his image that he wore a wig on the court. My mother, however, truth detective that she was, was not shocked. "Melissa, Andre Agassi was married to Brooke Shields, right?"

"Yes, he was. I know what you're thinking: if Brooke didn't mind that he's bald, why should he have had to worry about it? She's Brooke Shields!"

"Nice try, but that's not what I'm thinking. What I'm thinking is, since Andre was married to Brooke Shields, why spend all that money on high-end wigs and toupees? Why not just shave off one of Brooke's eyebrows and tape it to his head? It would've looked just as good, and he'll have saved a fortune. A win-win." And why, you ask, am I sharing this story? Because the bottom line is, image matters. Most show business images are created by well-respected, well-paid professionals, called "publicists," and they run Hollywood.

"Melissa, the first thing you need to do once you're getting established in Hollywood is get a good publicist. They'll make your career."

"Can I use your publicist?"

"Melissa, my precious, beautiful, wonderful daughter... of course not. My publicist develops *my* image; helping you would be a conflict of interest."

"How would helping me be a conflict of interest?"

"Hypothetically, let's say we're coming home from a big, star-studded, red carpet, Hollywood event. And somehow, right after we leave, our limousine gets in a car accident. No one's seriously hurt other than the driver, and let's be honest, he's not famous, so other than his wife, his parole officer, and his immigration lawyer, no one really cares about him. No one.

"Now listen carefully, my little one. The first thing I do, before calling 911, is call my publicist, who, faster than you can say, 'Slow the fuck down, it's a red light, you moron,' has every major news outlet on site, cameras everywhere. He makes sure that the story is 'Joan Rivers in car crash. Uses super-human strength to save daughter Melissa.'

"Then, I mess up my hair and dress and get out of the car to a sea of flashbulbs. I say, 'Thank God, Melissa's fine. She's just a little shook up, so she's staying in the car for now.' Then, I wipe a tear from my eye, and say, 'Let's pray that our wonderful driver has a full and speedy recovery, and I ask you to please respect our privacy at this time.' Then I look all pious and concerned as I crawl back into the car to comfort you."

"But what if that's not the truth?"

"Truth?! Truth doesn't matter, Melissa; no one will know. A few days after the crash, you'll release a statement saying you're grateful we're both okay and that you're blessed to have such a wonderful mother.

"And *that* is why we don't share a publicist."

"You just thought of this entire scenario now?"

Silence.

I was appalled but not shocked, kind of like when you turn on your TV set and see Rob Lowe starring in a different series on every single channel, including streaming services, all at the same time. Seriously, who's his agent?

"Missy, you know who taught me the value of publicity? Barbra Streisand. That girl is one smart cookie. Before she ever got an agent or a manager, she hired a publicist. She knew that getting a lot of press would make it easier for her to get a good agent and manager. And you've got to say, her plan worked: a hundred and thirty years after she started, she's still famous and relevant. Not only that, her PR team turned her flaws into assets."

"What flaws? She's one of the greatest singers, composers, directors, and actors of all time."

"The nose, Melissa, the nose. That whole story of how Barbra refused to get a nose job because she thought it would affect her voice is total spin. Babs's decision had nothing to with her being afraid of vocal repercussions, or some moral principle, but because in those days, the surgeons didn't have the technology to hack off something that size, without bringing in a chainsaw, a backhoe, and the Army Corps of Engineers.

"Her publicists managed to convince everyone that her giant nose was beautiful. They did this by having every photo feature her hands. That's because Barbra has gorgeous hands and beautiful long fingers. She would have made a fantastic pickpocket."

When the day came for me to finally hire my own publicist, my mother was actually generous with her advice. (I know what you're thinking. Was she drunk? Was she being blackmailed? Did she lose a bet?)

"Angelpuss, the most important things you need in a publicist are hunger, connections, and the ability to spin.

"Take hunger. You want a PR person who is still climbing up the food chain, looking to acquire clients, who can add a little cache to their portfolio."

"Don't I want the best publicist in Hollywood?"

"No."

"Why not?"

"Because you're not the best. And I don't mean that in a cruel, insensitive, Joan Crawford kind of way. What I mean is, the biggest PR flacks represent the biggest stars, and you'll never be their top priority. You want a rep who wakes up every day thinking, 'What can I do to get Melissa Rivers some good publicity today?'

"Think about Jeffrey Dahmer. He had a fabulous publicist: that guy was hungry; not hungry in the same way Jeffrey was, but you know what I mean. Without his PR guy, Dahmer was just another bland, run-of-the-mill, Midwestern, gay cannibal with a taste for dark meat. With his power PR team working 24/7, JD has not only become a legend in the world of maniacal serial killers, but he's a cottage industry as well! There are Dahmer T-shirts and hats and mugs, not to mention cookware, flatware, and storage bins. Pardon my choice of words, but the Dahmer brand is just killing. You know, for all his smarts, Ted Bundy was a dunce; Ted could've made a fortune if he knew anything about marketing, but no, he was too busy escaping and hiding in the woods. What are you gonna do? You can't fix stupid.

"Second big thing is connections. Not every publicist can get Steven Spielberg on the phone. But you don't need that. You need a publicist who can get Steven's brother, Norm, on the phone, and Norm's pretty good at relaying messages.

"Third is spin. You need someone who can turn an ugly situation into a winning hand, and who can turn tragedy into sunshine. Remember James Dean?"

"Of course. He died in a car crash when he was twenty-four. And now he's a legend."

"Right. And do you know how many films he made? Three. *Three!* That's only two more films than Abraham Zapruder made. But Dean's publicist turned him into an icon.

"Speaking of the Zapruder film, you know who had a great publicist? Jackie Kennedy. November 22, 1963. There they are in Dallas, in the motorcade. JFK gets shot in the head, blahblahblahblah. And there's that famous scene of Jackie climbing out on the trunk of the moving car. The story told to the public is that Jackie was heroically trying to help a secret service man get into the car to help the president. Not true. The real story was that she was trying to get out of the car to find some club soda because Jack's head had ruined her new, pink, five-thousand-dollar Chanel suit and matching pillbox hat. She didn't want to let the stain settle."

"Good to know, Mom, but how does this info help me? I don't ride in motorcades."

"It's about the power of the publicist, Melissa. The biggest PR success story in show biz was hiding the fact that Rock Hudson was gay. It was the biggest untold secret in Hollywood for years! Rock Hudson was so gay, he thought semen was one of the four basic food groups, yet some great publicists turned him into a movie star and leading man. Women all over the world were in love with him. When rumors started to circulate that Rock might be gay, they married him off to some woman to quiet things down. And for decades, it worked. And FYI, Rock's public relations people weren't dealing with the aftermath of a scandal or a tragedy; they knew Rock was gay right from the get-go. I mean, how could they not? His real name wasn't Rock Hudson; it was Cock Hudson."

Even though I knew a great deal of what my mother had told me was bullshit, I knew she was being honest about needing a good publicist if you're in show business. And when the time came, I hired my own PR firm...and they're great. And that's the truth. And if you don't believe me, ask my new boyfriend, Brad Pitt.

In my kitchen...a room we referred to as "the guest room." My mother looks so happy. This was taken right after she found out that Kathy Griffin's show had been canceled.

Who Are You Wearing?

In 1993, the E! television network called my mother and said, "Joan, would you like to host a pre-awards show for this year's Golden Globes?" She immediately said, "Yes!" It went so well that they called her again in 1994 and asked, "Joan, would you like to host *this* year's Golden Globe Awards pre-show?" And again, she immediately said, "Yes!" Then they said, "Would you like to host it along with your daughter, Melissa?" And she immediately said, "Who? And is it favored nations?"

Doing that first red carpet show together turned out to be huge—not just for me and my mother, but for the E! network, the movie studios, and the designers as well. Not to mention the movie stars and celebrities. *Live From the Red Carpet* became destination television; in many respects, it was far more entertaining than many of the awards shows themselves...not to mention, shorter. "Who are you wearing?" became a bigger Hollywood catchphrase than, "Who are you doing?" or, "Who are you paying off?" or, "Who's your plastic surgeon?"

I'm proud that my mom and I made the red carpet synonymous with Hollywood celebrity and glamour, and even prouder that the tradition we started carries on today. But I'm not so vain as to think that we invented the red carpet itself as a symbol of power and importance (although my mother would be so vain as to think that). I knew that the actual rolling out of the red carpet began long before my mother and I started badgering celebrities about their clothes, jewelry, and yeast infections. And, being the inquisitive spawn of a nosy parent, I did some investigating.

One year, during rehearsals for our pre-Oscar show, I said, "Mom, did you ever wonder how the red carpet itself came to be?" Before giving her a chance to lie or make up some bullshit story, I continued, "Well, I do. I was curious, so I did some research."

"That's why you're single, Melissa. Instead of waxing or powdering, you're researching. When is the last time you heard a man say, 'All I want is a woman with great research skills and a working knowledge of the Dewey Decimal System'? Never, that's when. And take off your glasses!"

Amazed as I was at how she managed to work my private life into a conversation about the red carpet, I remained nonplussed and continued. "Well, it turns out the rolling-out-the-red-carpet concept started thousands of years ago. In 458 BC (Before Cable), the Greek writer, Aeschylus, wrote *Agamemnon*. In the play, King Agamemnon returns home from winning a battle, and walks a 'crimson path' from his chariot to his home."

"Melissa, do you think I don't know the story of Agamemnon? I dated Aeschylus; lousy in bed and so hairy I didn't know if I was with a swarthy man or a feminist woman who refused to wax."

"Anyway, Mom, in ancient times, red was considered a color of power and strength...it signified dominance and class. It was the color of royalty. And the carpet wasn't always a carpet; sometimes, it was flower petals or cloth that had been dyed red..."

I could sense my mother was getting bored (she went for the Altoids, her "tell") because we weren't talking about things she liked—fame, fortune, or her. I realized I had to make the story more relevant...

"...cloth that had been dyed red because it was *cheaper* than buying actual red cloth or deep-pile fibers, which were very *expensive* and most often seen inside the king's castle, not outside on a common footpath." Her interest piqued by the prospect of discounts, I continued, "The red carpet not only showed the power of the throne, but kept the king's feet from touching the ground as well."

"I know a couple of queens whose feet never touch the ground—my hairdresser, my florist, and that eighty-year-old 'bachelor' who lives in apartment 6-J." (Just because it's a cheap joke, doesn't mean it's not funny; fuck off!)

"The whole 'red thing' carried on through the ages. The Catholic Church only allows their highest-ranking members, the cardinals and the pope, to wear red."

"I know that, Melissa, and it really, really bothers me, especially when this pope wears red. Everyone, with the apparent exception of his stylist, knows he shouldn't wear red—the man is clearly an autumn."

"Since then, presidents, world leaders, and corporate bigwigs all use red carpets when they make entrances, so it's only natural that the red carpet would eventually find its way to the Oscars and Hollywood royalty. Now, aren't you glad you asked?"

"Melissa, not only did I not ask, but what you said isn't accurate. Yes, Agamemnon walked the first red carpet, not because he was king, but because he was smart. His wife, Cheryl, was known for having had a notoriously heavy flow and he'd already had to replace two white carpets, with custom red key design borders. He wised up and the color scheme reversed. Time for rehearsal, let's go."

And the lying continues.

Fake It Till You Make It

Believe it or not, my mother was an optimist. Not in that preternatural, always sunny Kelly Ripa kind of way, more in a glass-half-full, pragmatic kind of way. In fact, she hated really chipper, upbeat people (not Kelly Ripa; she loved Kelly...more on that later). You know, the kind of people who see a house fire and think of it as both a good way to warm their hands and a jobs program for firefighters.

My mother had issues with people who were bubbly and happy for no apparent reason. For example, she could never quite understand Mr. Rogers's relentless joy and cheer.

"Melissa, how is it possible that Mr. Rogers is so happy all the time? Every single day, there he is, in that boring neighborhood, smiling and singing and telling uplifting stories. Every single day, the same fucking sweater; doesn't even try to accessorize. He's surrounded by children who are whining and picking their noses. I don't get it. The man must be heavily medicated. Maybe his milk and cookies are spiked with Valium."

"Mom..."

"I'll bet that's why he speaks so slowly. 'Good. Morning. Boys. And. Girls. How. Are. You. Today?' By the time he finishes saying 'good morning,' it's nighttime and the kids are either in bed sleeping or tied up in the back of a windowless van owned by a heavily armed drifter.

"And on another front, how come, in all those years, Mr. Rogers never once relocated, you know, moved on up, to the East Side, like the Jeffersons? He was on the air forever, made a ton of money, yet stayed put. Never upgraded to a bigger house in a better neighborhood? Who did he think he was, Warren Buffett? He could've gotten a house with a pool or a staff or a circular driveway—or at least something with more curb appeal. And if he didn't want to move, maybe it was for sentimental reasons ('This is where I raised my kids,' or, 'This is the house where we found Nana, dead in a pool of blood in the laundry room...'), then at least go for a little renovation? Put in a skylight. Bring in a tile guy to redo the countertops, something. But no, he did nothing, yet remained Mr. Rogers happy. He seemingly had no ambition, no taste, and a possible opioid problem. Go figure."

As I mentioned above, my mother loved Kelly Ripa. Kelly is naturally sweet and perky. It's not some TV contrivance or false face she puts on to sell a product line or a book or brand. She is real. My mom truly appreciated Kelly's honesty because, as you all know, if there's one thing my mother hated, it was a false face (one, *two*, *three*, *four*...insert plastic surgery joke here. Yes, the irony is obvious).

It's the same reason my mother loved celebrities like Kirstie Alley and Liz Taylor. They owned their shit. My mother could make millions of jokes about Kirstie or Liz and they never complained or whined...because they owned their fatness. Kirstie Alley even did a TV show called *Fat Actress*. As my mother said, "Kirstie got knocked down, but she got back up; it required six pulleys, a mule team, and some sort of hydraulics to do it, but by God, the woman got back up!" Which my mother loved.

"Melissa, if Kirstie didn't tell you she was having trouble finding work, you would never have known; she kept it to herself. Her public persona stayed the same, which is great, because studios and producers can smell desperation a mile away. Although in Kirstie Alley's case, that might not have been true; she smelled more of linguini, spaghetti, cheesecake, donuts, and pie. (You know, the way realtors bake bread in a house when they're trying to sell it.)"

My mother had a couple of expressions that she used to say to me over and over and over again: "Everyone gets knocked down in life; it's what you do when you get up that matters," and, "Always look forwards because if you look backward, you'll trip and fall," and, "I hear Mrs. Lindenbaum in the penthouse can shoot ping pong balls out of her pussy. Which is why she lives in the penthouse."

"Fake it till you make it" is another expression my mother loved. It's often said to people who are either struggling to get ahead or getting up after being knocked down. In Alcoholics Anonymous, they refer to that as "acting as if"—you know, act is if everything is fine and it eventually will be. (FYI, the only reason I bring up AA is because not only do I live less than five milligrams away from Promises Rehab in Malibu, but 43 percent of all the people I've ever worked with have millions of rewards points at the Betty Ford Center in Palm Springs.)

According to my mother, "Fake it till you make it" is not limited to business or career matters; in orgasms, to be specific. My orgasms, to be even more specific. My mother told me that it doesn't matter if a man is good in bed as long you let him think he is.

In Eve Ensler's play, *The Vagina Monologues*, one of the monologues is about the various kinds of moans a woman makes when having an orgasm. Turns out there are an operetta of moans. My mother and I went to see the play. Fourteen times. (She lied to get me there thirteen of those times. One time, I even thought we were going to the Super Bowl.) All through the play, my mother kept whispering, "Melissa, take notes. I can't be responsible for teaching you everything. You never know when you'll need to learn how to fake one of those moans. Besides which, if you take notes, the tickets are tax write-offs." I'm not sure which horrified me more, imagining my mother in bed, faking an orgasm, or the fact that she'd found a way to make moaning a tax loophole.

"Unfortunately, Missy, men can't fake orgasms. They actually have to get it up and fire the cannon. The only way a guy can fake it is to date blind women and smuggle bananas and tubes of toothpaste into bed. So, the burden of lying falls on us women."

"Mom...since when do you consider lying a burden?"

"When I'm on my back trying not to mess my hair or have my boobs slip under my arms, that's when. Wait till you get older and the creaking sound he hears isn't the mattress.

"Most men like three things in bed: reaching orgasm, reaching orgasm without working too hard, and reaching orgasm and not having to clean up or cuddle up. If they can satisfy the woman, fine, but it's not a priority. But if a man *thinks* he's satisfying you in bed, you'll get much better jewelry."

"Mom, women don't have sex with men because they want gifts. Technically, that would make every woman a prostitute."

"Yes, you are correct. Be honest, Melissa, if a man surprised you with an expensive Rolex after you gave him a mediocre blow job, you'd give it back? I don't think so."

"Mediocre?"

"I'm assuming. Let's be honest...it tastes disgusting. No wonder so many women are bulimic. I don't know why the homos love it so much; maybe it's a Keto thing.

"One of the first times I ever gave a blow job, the guy said to me, 'Where do you want me to come?' I said, 'The kitchen, and while you're there, could you get me a snack?'

"Let's get back on point. You're much better lying to him and saying things like, 'I want to see you climax,' or 'I've always wanted to visit Old Faithful.'

"And do not, I repeat, do *not* expect your 'lip service' to be reciprocal. Most men don't want to do it, don't know how to do it, and when they do do it, they make way too much noise. The slurping and lapping sounds? Disgusting. Sounds like a dog attacking a bowl of canned dog food."

"Canned dog food?"

"I could've name-checked a brand, but no one's offered me a product placement deal, so fuck 'em; canned dog food, it is."

"Great advice, Mom. Thanks."

"You're welcome, darling."

Continuing on, "If a man says, 'Am I the best?' The answer is 'no.'"

"What?"

"If you say 'yes,' it means you've fucked everyone else on the planet and he came in first place. So lie, because chances are, he's not the best. Men who are good in bed don't need to ask; they know. Not once did Clark Gable or George Clooney ever ask, 'Joan, was I the best?'"

I was about to call her out on the Gable and Clooney nonsense, but she didn't take a breath. "Al Roker never, ever, ever asked me to compare him with Willard Scott or Sam Champion."

"Wait a minute; you're telling me that you hooked up with Al Roker, Willard Scott, *and* Sam Champion?"

"Yes, Melissa, I did, although I think Sam Champion was only in it so he could borrow my heels. Willard had this odd fetish; we'd be in the middle of everything and he'd keep shouting out, 'How old are you? How old are you?' and I'd shout back something like, 'Today's my birthday, and I'm a hundred and three years young!' Al Roker liked to play games too; his favorite was the one where I'm in a Kansas cornfield and he's a big stormfront passing through. Sam loved to watch that one because it reminded him of *The Wizard of Oz*...and, you know...Judy."

"What do you mean, 'Sam liked to watch?' Sam was there? Please tell me you did not do a three-way with Sam and Al!"

"What can I say, Melissa? I'm a sucker for meteorologists. Anyway, what I'm trying to impart to you is that faking an orgasm is a perfectly good lie. Think about it; the man feels great about himself and his performance, and you've had a chance to work on your acting skills. It's a win-win!"

"I never thought of it like that."

"Sure, it's the ultimate acting class. Strasberg Technique in action. If you think Meryl Streep can act on screen, you should see her in bed. A masterclass."

"How would you know what Meryl Streep does in be— Oh, God, not her too?"

"I'll never tell. Not only do loose lips sink ships; they can sink Oscar winners' careers too. So, Missy, next time you're with a man and he's no good in bed, moan, tell him how special he is, and then go in the bathroom and let the shower head do for you what he couldn't. You know, fake it till you make it."

How to Lie in Hollywood

In 1954, Darrell Huff wrote a bestselling book called *How to Lie with Statistics*, which is still considered a classic by people who are a) fond of statistics, and/or b) fond of lying. It was one of my mother's favorite books (it was actually on her nightstand, along with *Gray's Anatomy*, *The Merck Manual of Diagnosis and Therapy*, the *Kama Sutra*, and *In Cold Blood*) and you can probably figure out if she was a member of group a) or b). Surprisingly, it was a breezy, illustrated read that explained how to lie to your advantage by using statistics, graphs, and comparisons.

My mother used this book as source matter to help her learn (and teach me) how to lie in show business.

"Melissa, in show business, bending the truth is the way of the world. It is the oxygen that feeds the fire of the entertainment industry. It is the seed from which all successful ventures grow. It's the jizz in the nut sack of life."

"If you want to have a good career in show biz, you need to learn some simple harmless lies.

"If you're at a show biz party, it is *always* appropriate to say to an actor or actress, 'I love your work.' Because even though you may be lying, you may be also half telling the truth. Let's say you're at a Hollywood party and you go outside to look for Tom Sizemore, who owes you money. (Maybe you lent him a hundred to pay a fine he got for taking a leak in a dumpster near a playground.) While looking for Tom, you run into a celebrity whose fame is inexplicable, let's call her Snookie. You give the Snookster a big hug and say, 'So good to see you! I *love* your show.'

"Then there's the dilemma of 'what to do' when you're at a party and you run into a famous celebrity and can't remember who the fuck they are."

"Has that ever happened to you?"

"Has that ever happened to me? That always happens to me, mostly because when I'm talking to a celebrity, I'm not always paying attention because I'm scanning the room to see if there's someone more important than they are who I need to suck up to.

"One time, I was at a fundraiser at Danny Thomas's house. I was in the den wiping down the glass coffee table when in walks Sidney Poitier. I was at a loss for words. I was both starstruck and hammered, and I couldn't put two thoughts together, so all I kept saying was, 'I love your work, I love your work.' After five minutes of this, Sidney had had enough and started backing out the door. He was just about out of the room and I yelled, 'Love your work, Mr. Poitier!'

"Sidney stopped, turned, and came back into the room. 'Mr. Poitier? Did you call me, Mr. Poitier?'

"'Why yes, I did. I thought that was only proper; I don't know you well enough to call you Sidney.'

"'Sidney? Did you call me Sidney?'

"'Yes, why? I thought...'

"'Because I'm Michelle Pfeiffer, you fucking dunce. What the fuck is wrong with you?'"

Another approved lying tactic in Hollywood is cozying up to a celebrity by making up and dishing dirt on a celebrity friend they can't stand. For example, the first time my mother met First Lady Nancy Reagan. Nancy was known for being a little aloof and my mother was afraid she'd be intimidated by her. They were introduced at a formal tea in Beverly Hills, very fancy shmancy—crumpets and biscuits and those tiny little finger sandwiches made with cucumbers and shrimp that nobody really likes. As my mother said later, "If this event was any more gentile, the tables and chairs would have foreskin." Anyway, during the course of the day, my mother found herself alone with Nancy in the ladies' room. As they were checking their hair and reapplying their makeup, my mother said, "I'm glad Barbara Bush isn't here. Rumor has it, she's very gassy."

Nancy smiled and said, "Around the White House, her nickname is the West Wind."

From that explosive moment on, my mom became friends with Nancy Reagan and even got invited to the White House—which, my mother says, is *very* hard to steal from. (Yet, somehow, she managed to "obtain" the original copy of the *Magna Carta*—which she used as a drying mat in the kitchen.)

"Melissa, the most impressive part of lying in Hollywood happens at the Oscars, when the winners are announced and the cameras immediately pan to the losers, who have to act happy for the winners. Which is, of course, total bullshit. There's no way Glenn Close can sit there, time after time, year after year, losing to one actress after another, and honestly be happy for all of them. Oh sure, she has a smile on her rather oddly masculine face, but down deep, she feels the pain from the bottom of her heart to the top of her balls. But Glenn always smiles, graciously. That's more than acting, that's lying. In my opinion, she should receive an Oscar for those performances. Best Losing Performance by an Actress Year after Year after Year.

"The other great, nonverbal Oscar lies occur during the presentation of the Dead Reel."

"The Dead Reel?"

"Yes, Melissa, the Dead Reel. You know, the 'In Memoriam' tape they run featuring all of the show biz people who died during that year. This nonverbal lying is determined by applause levels and audience shots."

"What the hell are you talking about?"

"Oh, for God's sake, Missy, pay attention! Everyone knows that all of the really big applause goes to the biggest stars, child stars, stars who died too young, or stars who died in accidents, overdoses, mishaps, or murders. The acting/lying part comes in when midrange dead stars appear on screen, you know, like Jack Klugman or Divine. People in the audience don't know how much to clap, or whether or not to clap at all. You don't want to over-clap or you'll look like a Needy Nelly looking for approval, and you don't want to not clap, because that bit of silence is reserved for the writers, animators, and other backstage deadies no one really cares about. So, my suggestion is, watch the in-house monitors: if Meryl claps, you clap; if Meryl cries, you cry.

"The real acting/lying part comes when the dead star on screen had more baggage than Louis Vuitton. Imagine that Mel Gibson dies—as many people in Boca Raton probably do. What do you do? Mel is a wonderful actor and great director and filmmaker. But he also had that alleged anti-Semitic, racist, neo-Nazi thing going on. So, here's my take on that: you don't clap, but you don't boo, either. You fold your hands in your lap, put a sad-yet-wistful look on your face, and shake your head slightly in a display of confused grief. Then sigh."

"What the fuck is a sad-yet-wistful look? How do I practice that?"

"Simple. Imagine you find out in public that your ex-boyfriend and his new twenty-year-old Russian model girlfriend were hit by a car. (Pause) Easy-peasy!"

I was speechless. My jaw dropped slightly, and my head tilted a little to the left. I let out a little sigh and my mother said, "That's it, Melissa! Perfect! Sad-yet-wistful. You're going to do great in show business! You're not only my favorite daughter, you're my favorite liar!"

Drowning in the Gene Pool

Genetics play an interesting role in our development and behavior. For example, Cooper looks like a combination of me and John. Individually, he doesn't resemble either one of us, but if we all stand together, he's clearly our son. He's inherited John's blue eyes and quiet reserve and my sense of humor and wonderment. And by wonderment, I mean he never stopped asking questions. Why this, why that, why him, why her? (I was in awe of many things, but not particularly interested in how they came to be.)

When Cooper was little, this quest for information was cute. When he got older, not so much. All day, all night. It was exhausting trying to come up with answer after answer after answer—like being on *Jeopardy!* and every category is Physics and Latin.

I couldn't imagine where Cooper's relentless inquisitiveness came from. He didn't get it from John, who only asked questions about horses' breeding patterns and my spending habits, and he didn't get it from me—I rarely asked actual questions because I knew most of my mother's answers wouldn't be true.

With nothing but time on my hands and white wine on the counter, I decided to investigate why Cooper was such a persistent...um...er...let's go with "seeker." I went online and joined 23andMe, so I could learn about our heritage and ancestry timeline to find out if there were any genetic components to our behaviors. Honestly, I only wanted to know about *his* background, but unless I made it into a "we" activity there was zero chance he would agree to giving me a DNA sample. (Which he actually didn't; one night I swabbed his drinking glass when he left the dinner table, and pulled hair from his brush when he was out on a date with some girl I assumed was way beneath him on the relationship food chain.)

I never wanted to do an ancestry test for myself, for fear that it would prove conclusively that my mother really was my mother, and that any waning hopes I had that I'd been adopted, kidnapped, or fallen from a truck would be dashed.

Truth be told, 23andMe is pretty amazing; they can tell you not just about your heritage, but about your nutritional and physical histories, your familial health history and tendencies; they can even tell you if you're predisposed to having a lot of earwax. Imagine if 23andMe existed centuries ago; is it possible that Beethoven wasn't really deaf, he just had lots of earwax and no Q-tips?

Anyway, the results of the DNA testing came back the day of the first big Thanksgiving dinner I hosted after my mother died. It showed there was no genetic evidence that Cooper was inquisitive for any reason other than his being highly intelligent. Even more important, there was no definitive evidence that I had inherited my mother's penchant for lying. Whew!

With this newfound knowledge, a light bulb suddenly went off. I finally understood the lying thing and realized why my mother told me so many stories that were just plain not true: she was bored of explaining things to me and making up tall tales was simply more fun.

Cooper and I were setting the table for our thirty-six guests (thirty-seven if the Rothmans brought their hirsute, spinster daughter Deborah, who wore corrective shoes out of spite, not necessity) when I noticed he kept switching the place cards all around, changing the seating assignments.

"Cooper, what are you doing? I very carefully put together a seating chart, so everybody would have a good time."

"Grandma told me making last minute switches was a tradition started by the Pilgrims at the first Thanksgiving, when one of the Pilgrim matrons switched up Mrs. Squanto's seat assignments because Mrs. Squanto knew nothing of table talk or conversational flow."

"Cooper, Grandma was lying; she made that up."

"Why would she do that?"

"I don't know, Cooper; why do dogs chase cats? They just do. But, if you want to know the real story of the first Thanksgiving, I'll be happy to tell you."

"Okay, Mom. But you'll tell me the truth?"

"Of course, I will, Cooper! Would I lie to you? Who do you think I am, Grandma?"

Cooper sat down, smiled that million-dollar smile of his, put his elbows up on the table, and eagerly began to listen.

"Well, Cooper, it was 1952, in Fort Lauderdale, Florida. The Norwegian Princess ship had just come in from an eight-day, nine-night cruise of the Bahamas, carrying a full load of mostly Jewish passengers, all headed to Boca Raton..."

Epilogue

I'm glad I wrote this book after my mother had died. Can you imagine the conversation we would have had if I wrote this while she was still here...?

"Mom, guess what? That book deal I've been working on came through!"

"I know."

"What do you mean you know?"

"Margie told me."

"How does Margie know?'

"I don't know."

"How did she know I was working on a book deal? I told you not to tell anyone."

"I didn't!"

"Did you tell Margie?"

"Of course, I told Margie; she's my best friend."

"I told you not to tell *anyone*!"

"I didn't."

Acknowledgments

First, I want to thank my co-author, Larry Amoros; your ability to completely ignore the truth explains why you've been part of our family for years. Thanks to Post Hill and our wonderful editor Wenonah Hoye, who managed to keep the crazy train on the tracks; you're the best. Thanks to Tom Flannery for his great agenting. (Is "agenting" actually a word?) I'm eternally grateful for the love and support of so many wonderful, loyal, and amazing people. I would name-check all of you, but I know I'll forget some of you and I don't have the bandwidth to deal with any more drama right now. Have you watched the news lately? 'Nuff said. For anyone else who would traditionally be acknowledged in this section, consider yourself thanked. And to the rest of you...I could lie some more, but honestly it's become exhausting.

For Melvin,
I'm prettier.

About the Author

Melissa Rivers is a celebrated, award-winning television personality and producer, as well as a *New York Times* bestselling author. She is also vice president of foreign affairs for the government of Peru in addition to being one of the founding fathers of the United States of America. She is the loving mother of a twenty-one-year-old son, Cooper, and the not-so-loving mother of two triplets she sold on the black market for whiskey and smokes in desperate times. There are moments she regrets that decision, but thankfully, they pass.

For more information...on second thought, that's more than enough.